I0790457

Transformational and Transactional Leadership in Mental Health and Substance Abuse Organizations

Dr. B.G. Nash Sr., PhD, ThD

TRANSFORMATION AND TRANSACTIONAL LEADERSHIP IN MENTAL HEALTH AND SUBSTANCE ABUSE ORGANIZATIONS

iUniverse books may be ordered through booksellers or by contacting:

iUniverse
1663 Liberty Drive
Bloomington, IN 47403
www.iuniverse.com
844-349-9409

Because of the dynamic nature of the Internet, any web addresses or links contained in this book may have changed since publication and may no longer be valid. The views expressed in this work are solely those of the author and do not necessarily reflect the views of the publisher, and the publisher hereby disclaims any responsibility for them.

Any people depicted in stock imagery provided by Getty Images are models, and such images are being used for illustrative purposes only.
Certain stock imagery © Getty Images.

ISBN: 978-1-6632-3747-7 (sc)
ISBN: 978-1-6632-3754-5 (hc)
ISBN: 978-1-6632-3748-4 (e)

Library of Congress Control Number: 2022905358

Print information available on the last page.

iUniverse rev. date: 06/03/2022

CONTENTS

PREFACE

Mental health counselors and managers play central roles in guiding recovery strategies for substance abuse disorders. In particular, the communication between the counselor and manager plays a central role in guiding ideal patient quality and care. Significant research exists regarding leadership models, skills, and traits. However, when exploring the leadership models of mental health counselors and managers for substance abuse facilities, research is absent. Further, research regarding the efficacy of transformational and transactional leadership styles for mental health counselors and managers was absent in the reviewed literature.

As such, the purpose of this qualitative research was to explore how transactional and transformational leadership influence the counselor and manager relationship in mental health counseling settings. The guiding research questions explored the transformational and transactional managerial tactics that produced positive work outcomes and relationships between the counselor and the managers. The data collection model included conducting semi-structured interviews with ten counselors and ten managers from two counseling offices in New York City. The interviews were subsequently transcribed and thematically analyzed. Key emergent themes included the perception of transformational leadership style as more effective than transactional leadership style. Implications for employee effectiveness and increasing employee outcomes and behavior were elucidated. Recommendations for practice included a focus toward transformational leadership for productivity, employee retention, and increasing employee morale for leadership within mental health facilities.

CHAPTER 1

Introduction

Leadership skills are the primary focus for success in many organizations and are necessary to remain competitive (Tang, 2019). Researchers have placed special emphasis on how leadership develops a certain amount of influence through leadership personality, inspirational motivation, and individual considerations (Saravo, Netzel, & Kiesewetter, 2017). Recent research has primarily focused on leadership styles, such as transformational and transactional leadership styles. These studies typically focused on the impact of leadership styles on employees and organizational goals (Kark, Van Diijk, & Vashdi, 2018).

The focus of this book is on the impact of leadership styles of mental health and substance abuse managers toward their subordinate counselors. Specifically, this researcher aimed to explore the effects of transformational and transactional leadership styles on relationships between the counselor and manager. First, broad research regarding organizational practices and the implementation of evidence-based practices for employees who work with substance abuse disorders, including alcohol and drug abuse, is reviewed within this chapter. Traditionally, researchers focus on the role of leadership toward patients rather than the counselor and manager relationship (Guerrero, Frimpong, & Kong, 2019). However, this researcher addressed the problem that transformational and transactional leadership of counseling managers has not been studied. Additionally, it is unclear if they are benefiting from these methods.

The larger context of this study is that the current body of academic literature typically focused on the use of transactional and transformational leadership to further organizational progress (Cho, Shin, Billing, & Bhagat, 2019). Current researchers focus on the attributes and qualities of leaders that are needed to achieve organizational goals (Sosik & Jung, 2018). However, research focusing on the impact of leadership qualities toward subordinates is lacking. Furthermore, research that examines the relationship of leadership styles within mental health substance abuse organizations (e.g., counselors and managers) is understudied.

This research is relevant and warranted because leadership is vital to providing direction to employees and creating a shared understanding of professionalism within an industry. A recent study by Andersen, Bjørnholt, Bro, and Holm-Petersen (2018) noted that the interactions between transformational leadership, performance, and professionalism are seldom investigated. Andersen et al. further argued that as a result, little is understood concerning the ability for transformational leadership styles to assist in the creation of mutual understandings (e.g., professionalism) between employees and leaders. Their remarks illustrate how transformational leadership shared concepts between peers is useful. However, the author directed his argument toward childcare counselors, not toward the mental health and substance abuse industry.

Expert studies cross a wide range of industries such as health care, education, business, and social sciences. Within the health care field, leadership studies are aimed at organizational practices, improving counselor interactions with clients or patients, or developing methods to provide cost-effective training for counselors involved with the direct care of individuals diagnosed with mental disorders and substance use disorders.

Previous research has been conducted on organizational leadership (Breevaart & Bakker, 2018). This topic is practical as leadership qualities are the focus of improving organizational and employee productivity. It is equally important to study human phenomena within relationships when trying to make positive changes in an organization and its employees. However, when studies are limited to the relationship between manager and organization, or between counselor and clients, gaps in research are created. The relationship between counselor and manager is either omitted or unavailable in the current body of research related to leadership methods. As such, the theoretical framework of transactional and transformation leadership will be used to frame this study. Transactional and transformational leadership theories frame the current problem and explore the possible effect of managers who use these leadership styles with their subordinate counselors.

Currently, there is no available literature concerning the leadership of managers with their counselors. However, there is related research about the relationship between the manager and the counselor. For example, Holman, Watts, Robles-Pina, and Grubbs (2018) studied counselor burnout and associated methods for ameliorating burnout by managers.

Similarly, Schilling, Randolph, and Boan-Lenzo (2018) found that managers utilize several tactics to combat counselor burnout, including peer advice, team management training, and offering personal advice. They noted that burnout is acknowledged by managers, who also typically provide assistance. Burnout could include unexpected work difficulties. One of these includes job overload, when a counselor takes on more than he or she can handle (Schilling et al., 2018).

Similar research by Quintana and Cabrera (2015) focused on counseling organizations rather than on counselor and manager relationships. They found that organizations typically focus on improving services, client satisfaction, and employee productivity. However, Holman et al., Schilling et al., and Quintana and Cabrera did not examine the impact of transformational and transactional leadership styles on the counselor and manager relationship.

Within the business field, researchers measured the performance of each leadership style to determine the most effective leadership style to promote a positive influence on employees (Sheshi & Kercini, 2017). Problematically, leadership researchers are mostly concerned with organizational issues, such as how to become more qualified for internships or how to improve services according to government policies. These studies fail to consider frontline personnel who serve to implement new strategies. As such, organization and employee satisfaction are at the center of business researchers rather than the impact of leadership on counselors (Mujkic, Sehic, Rahimic, & Jusic, 2014).

Other forms of leadership research, such as educational leadership research, have focused on evaluating transformational leadership in enhancing the classroom experience (Pounder, 2014). These studies provide valuable information for the education sector. However, they do not provide information for the specific field of counseling (e.g., Mujic et al., 2014).

A few researchers have investigated job-related variables about counseling. For example, Wardle and Mayorga (2016) examined the indicators of job burnout for counselors, but the authors did not provide recommendations regarding leadership supports, such as transactional or transformational styles. The authors did provide recommendations regarding self-care and wellness. Wardle and Mayorga also mentioned health peer supervisors, which allowed managers to trade ideas. Ideally, these health peer supervisors would aid in the development of efficient counselors and build a positive work ethic. The topic of health peer superiors is an excellent example of the opportunity to examine the effect of transformational or transactional leadership on the work performance of counselors in direct contact with individuals with mental disorders and/or substance abuse. Wardle and Mayorga did not, however, explore transactional or transformational leadership in their discussion of health peer supervisors. This problem can be addressed by the present study because it documents the relationship of managers' leadership styles and their effects on the counselors, providing managers with information about effective tactics. The transactional leadership tactic is characterized by a give-and-take relationship between counselors and managers.

Transformational leadership is known for its four tactics—inspirational, positive motivation, building self-confidence, and allowing the follower to visualize the purpose of his or her work progress. This study documents the use of each and their effects on counselor productivity.

Statement of the Problem

The problem this study addressed is that although there is significant research on leadership within the business setting (Smith & Khojasteh, 2014), there is a gap in the literature regarding the leadership relationship between counselors and managers in the mental health field (Bowen & Moore, 2014). There is significant research regarding transactional and transformational leadership in business and education (Smith & Khojasteh, 2014) and assessments regarding relationships between the leader and the subordinate (Esty & Bell, 2018). Yet how transformational and transactional leadership styles among mental health office managers affect the relationships between counselor and managers in professional relationships is not yet known.

Relationships between counselors and managers impact professional relationships and the services provided by counselors (Saravo, Netzel, & Kiesewetter, 2017). Researchers indicated that the relationship between counselors and managers reinforces the efforts, work ethics, and professionalism of the counselor, allowing the counselor to help the client improve (Muchiri, McMurray, Nkhoma, & Pham, 2019). Research found a lack of communication between counselor and manager impacts services provided (Morrison & Lent, 2018), and according to researchers Clipa and Greciuc (2018), the relationship between counselor and manager impacts client success.

This gap in research indicated the need for further research to examine how transformational and transactional leadership styles influence counselor and manager relationships in a mental health and substance abuse setting. The proposed qualitative research fills this gap by investigating the use and associated impact of transformational and transactional leadership styles in the mental health field. This information may impact the overall effectiveness of both the manager and the counselor in their respective job duties.

Purpose of the Study

The purpose of this qualitative research was to explore how transactional and transformational leadership influence the counselor and manager relationship in mental health counseling settings. Previous researchers focused on leadership in business and educational settings for the betterment of the organization. Research regarding mental health and substance abuse counselors and their managers is absent in academic literature.

This study is a logical response to the problem of the lack of understanding of how transformational and transactional leadership styles are used by managers of mental health counselors. These issues lead to research questions that are focused on how the transformational and transactional managerial methods are used in the counselor and manager relationship, how they impact that relationship, and the outcomes of those methods.

Methodology for this study was qualitative with a thematic design. The data collation used in-depth, one-on-one interviews to uncover which leadership type was used, which style—if any—dominated, and what counselors felt was appropriate to improve work progress and attitudes toward leadership.

Counselors and managers interviewed indicated which leadership style or styles they used. Constructs consisted of two types of leadership styles. First is transformational, which is inspirational and motivational. Second is transactional, which is a give-and-take type of interaction (Andersen, Bjørnholt, Bro, & Holm-Petersen, 2018).

The target population was counselors who work with mental health and substance abuse clients and their immediate managers. All interviews were held in the local library or a conference room, with permission from the necessary authoritative individuals. The sampling frame consisted of approximately ten counselors and ten managers who volunteered from a total population of fifty counselors and managers working at a total of two counseling offices in the New York City region.

Data was gathered via an audio-recording device and handwritten notes. Data was analyzed using thematic analysis. To assist in the study, NVivo qualitative software was used to evaluate data patterns found in sentences and paragraphs. These coded similarities in the textual evidence were used to construct themes, which were used in addressing the research questions and the problem statement. This helped to identify which leadership type is beneficial in the counselor and manager relationship.

Theoretical/Conceptual Framework

The conceptual framework was the theories of transactional and transformational leadership. Leadership was defined as a general conceptual framework and detailed the conceptual frameworks of transactional and transformational leadership that guided this study.

The conceptual framework of leadership is to ensure that jobs are done efficiently (Kang & Svensson, 2018). This behavior by managers is defined as having the ability to influence followers, which aids in accomplishing work objectives within an organization (Epitropaki, Kark, Mainemelis, & Lord, 2017). Communication between counselor and manager consists of facial expressions and body language, which is important in the relationship between counselor and manager (Nazim, 2016). This communication can be nonverbal, which is also important to the relationship between counselor and manager.

The concept of leadership is evaluated from many perspectives, including social, logical, organizational, and psychological (Vänni, Neupane, & Nygård, 2017). The social approach toward followers is viewed as more of a transactional type due to the authority the leader presents to get more productivity from followers. This relates to follower perceptions about leaders who place organizational needs before follower needs.

Three concepts related to leadership are transformational leadership, transactional leadership, and job satisfaction (Nazim, 2016). The transformational leadership approach pays attention to the follower by developing a teamwork environment, which encourages—transforms—followers to support each other (Nazim, 2016). In any organization where competition exists, the transformational leadership tactic helps bring positive innovations to the organization. According to Nazim, transformational leadership allows smooth changes within the organization through vision and encouragement, which is comprised of inspiration, charisma, intellectual stimulation, and individual consideration.

In contrast, the goal of transactional leadership is getting followers to work to earn compensation. Transactional leadership enhances the motivation of followers by offering rewards. If an assignment is not completed, there may be some negative consequences. The behavior of managers can influence job satisfaction whether it is negative or positive (Nazim, 2016).

The theories of transactional and transformational leadership methods were appropriate for developing the problem that despite significant research on leadership within the business setting (Smith & Khojasteh, 2014), there is a gap in the literature regarding the leadership relationship between counselors and managers in the mental health field (Bowen & Moore, 2014). As such, these theories were appropriate for developing the problem because each theory is an integral part of leadership research, though there is a lack of understanding of how they are applied in the setting of mental health care counselors and managers. Additionally, the theories of transactional and transformational were appropriate for developing the purpose of exploring how transactional and transformational leadership impact the counselor and manager relationship in mental health counseling settings. It is important to understand how these theories are used within the counseling and managerial settings of mental health settings to better understand how these leadership tactics may influence organizational goals (e.g., meeting the needs of patients). The theories of transactional and transformational leadership were appropriate for developing the research questions regarding how each managerial style produces positive relationships and work outcomes between the counselor and the manager because it directly addresses the noted problem and purpose statement. As such, the research questions served to further the understanding of these leadership theories while addressing the gap and the noted purpose statement.

Nature of the Study

Qualitative methodology facilitates the exploration of a particular phenomenon. Qualitative research is a text-based collection and analysis of data that seeks to understand the meanings people make from their daily lives regarding a topic of interest. Qualitative descriptive research design uses a variety of data sources that ensures the phenomena are explored through more than one lens (Lambert & Lambert, 2012). This procedure ensures the topic of interest is thoroughly examined and the phenomena revealed. The phenomena of interest were evaluated by the data collected through a semi-structured interview. Data was collected by using audio, video, or handwritten reports. Data gathered by audio or video was transcribed for analysis. Data analysis determined the patterns in the responses of the interview. The selected research methodology and design were the best choices for the study because they allow the researcher to understand the phenomena being studied, such as how transactional and transformational leadership affect job satisfaction, effective work, and ethics.

The qualitative descriptive approach was the appropriate choice as research involving humans and their interactions with others in a natural setting allows more objective research findings (Cristancho, Goldszmidt, Lingard, & Watling, 2018). The benefits of using a qualitative descriptive approach are that there are questions that require a one-to-one or group gathering. As Cristancho and associates found, these methods allow researchers to more accurately evaluate respondents' nonverbal responses and reactions to questions than if gathered through surveys. The qualitative method aligns with the problem of this study, which is the relationship between manager and follower because it is necessary to ask the managers and the followers, in this case counselors, about their relationships. Using interviews allowed the researcher to develop a rich understanding of that relationship.

Qualitative descriptive also aligned with another purpose of this study, which was to add to the already existing and limited research concerning relationships between counselors and managers in a mental health and substance abuse setting. The purpose of the study was to collect an understanding of these relationships, and therefore, qualitative descriptive interviews enable the collection of rich answers to specific questions about this relationship, as well as careful documentation of the themes across several participants.

Research Questions

RQ1: From the perspective of counselors and managers, what transformational managerial tactics produce positive work outcomes?

RQ2: From the perspective of counselors and managers, what transformational managerial tactics produce positive relationships between the counselor and the manager?

RQ3: From the perspective of counselors and managers, what transactional managerial tactics produce positive work outcomes?

RQ4: From the perspective of counselors and managers, what transactional managerial tactics produce positive relationships between the counselor and the manager.

Significance of the Study

The proposed research is important as it allowed the researcher to explore leadership types in mental health settings to find if and how managers are using the two types of leadership: transactional and transformational (Saravo et al., 2017). The results contributed to the current research by expanding the lens of transactional and transformational leadership from business to mental health management. The research also expanded current research on transformational and transactional leadership that focuses on the organization, such as counselor caseloads and maintaining a certain number of clients, and extended this to the relationship between counselor and manager (Begum, Begum, Rustam, & Rustam, 2018).

The study added to existing research on leadership because transformational and transactional leadership style qualities are part of the human phenomenon. A qualitative approach was sufficient in understanding how our society learns and what makes transactional or transformational leadership influential (Afsar, Badir, Saeed, & Hafeez, 2017).

Researchers concerned with this phenomenon may present a broader view of how leadership qualities, such as inspirational and intellectual (transformational) or a (transactional), give and take to improve work productivity. This researcher intended to find the underpinning elements of such leadership qualities, which were examined through empirical research of Breevaart and Bakker (2018). They also stated that the negative consequences of not attempting to find such factors may limit the understanding of the potential qualities of transformational and transactional leadership and the effect on counselors.

Definitions of Key Terms

Transformational leadership. According to Breevaart and Bakker (2018), transformational leadership is a tactic used by managers to enhance work performance by inspiring followers through the vision of the manager. Transformational leadership develops trust among followers and improves work performance (Muchiri, McMurray, Nkhoma, & Pham, 2019).

Transactional leadership. Transformational leadership is concerned with the success of the organization rather than teamwork (Clipa & Greciuc, 2018). Transactional leadership can be viewed as contingent rewards given by managers when followers complete organizational goals. Transactional leadership monitors followers' goals to take corrective action (Duemer, 2017).

Organizational outcome. In a study conducted by Saravo and Kiesewetter (2017), research found organizational outcome was enhanced for transactional leadership when followers' responsibilities were made clear for specific tasks, and transformational leadership followers were able to show appreciation for good efforts.

Manager. In transformational leadership, the relationship between manager and follower is based on the influence of the manager. Saravo, Netzel, and Kiesewetter (2017) found that when the manager expresses a vision of what the organization stands for and provides positive motivation for the follower, transactional leadership is based on individual accomplishments rather than team accomplishments. With transactional leadership, the relationship relies on contingent rewards and contractual obligations.

Summary

The key points that were discussed began with the premise that leadership skills are the primary focus for success in many organizations and are necessary to remain competitive (Saravo et al., 2017). Much of the research on leadership skills, such as transformational and transactional leadership styles, is concerned with how employees or followers are impacted by the influence of leadership. The next topic of the discussion of the problem was that while there is research on leadership within the business setting (Smith & Khojasteh, 2014), there is a gap in the literature regarding the leadership relationship between counselors and managers in the mental health field (Bowen & Moore, 2014).

The overall goal is to create a better understanding of how transactional and transformational leadership impact the counselor and manager relationship in mental health counseling settings. An examination of the theoretical framework was considered because it is the guiding framework that has been identified as leadership styles. The concept of leadership is to ensure counselors perform their jobs efficiently (Nazim, 2016).

How the research will expand previous research regarding transformational and transactional leadership is also included in this book. In summary, this book outlines a study that investigates transactional and transformational leadership styles in a mental health setting and how they affect counselors and managers.

CHAPTER 2

~~~

Literature Review

</div>

The purpose of this study was to fill the gaps in research concerning how transactional and transformational leadership influence the working relationship between counselor and manager. They may benefit from applying findings from other fields to the counselor and manager field. Current studies on leadership are aimed toward educational and business organizations and geared toward the betterment of such organizations. However, research regarding the use of transactional and transformational leadership within mental health and substance abuse practices are lacking in academic literature. This study is a response to that lack of research.

This chapter is organized into four main subsections, with the largest being the literature review itself. First, a discussion of search databases and terms is presented. Following the search database discussion, an analysis of the theory of social interaction is presented. This section connects the theory of social interaction to the purpose of this study. Next, the first section of the literature review discusses general definitions of
~~~

leadership, traits, and skills. This section laid the foundation for seminal works concerning the use of leadership, definition of leadership, and applicability of leadership styles.

Following this section, transformational and transactional leadership are each defined according to current literature. Transactional and transformational leadership are directly related to the purpose of this study, and this section outlines their definitions and critically analyzes their applications in current academic literature. The final two sections focus on critically analyzing and reviewing the previous applications of transformational and transactional leadership styles in business and health care fields. This is because the primary research on transformational and transactional leadership styles comes from those fields. It is assumed in this study that these two leadership styles are also applicable to the counseling management venue.

The first section, concerning transformational and transactional leadership in business organizations, is designed to provide an understanding of how these styles have benefited leaders, managers, and organizations. Finally, a section on leadership studies in health care discusses how these two leadership styles have adapted to the needs of health care leaders. Few studies exist regarding the leadership styles of mental health care managers. However, those addressing these managers will be included within this section on leadership in health care. A subsection is devoted to discussing current academic research regarding the applications of transactional and transformational leadership to various organizations. The final section is a summary of the reviewed literature as it applies to purpose of this study.

The following search databases were used to locate literature relevant to the purpose of this study: *Google Scholar, ProQuest, EBSCO, JSTOR, PubMed,* and *ERIC Database.* All the search terms relevant to the topic and contents were used to search for articles and books. Range of years used for the research was five years, 2015 to 2019. From this literature review, 105 sources were peer-reviewed. A total of nine books were used to provide foundational definitions concerning leadership. One dissertation was utilized due to the relevancy of the information provided from the research. Relevant literature was primarily peer-reviewed. Non-peer-reviewed sources were seminal research related to the topic of leadership.

Theory of Social Interaction

The theoretical framework selected for this study is that of social interaction. The theory of social interaction was developed by Gary Becker in 1974 as a framework to guide economic explorations of social interactions within the consumer-demand market. According to Becker's original framework, each person is part of social relationships that affect his or her behavior. In this way, people are influenced by other people. Someone in the system of social relationships is a leader, a follower, or within the liminal space of these two categories. Becker based his theory within the ideology that all individuals are inherently social and desire to have some form of social interaction with others. However, these social interactions influence a variety of social aspects and influence the perception of that individual based on his or her actions and reactions in social interactions.

Social interaction theory and the place of an individual within the theory allow for the adoption of new ideas and changes. Additionally, informal contacts are no less important than formal relationships; new phenomena are gradually spreading in the team (Antonakis & Day, 2017). Considering this theory, according to Antonakis and Day, an experienced leader will first test a new idea on the leaders of public opinion in the organization. If accepted by supporters, leaders will be able to acquaint others with their ideas and convince them of their expediency. Additionally, leaders should be familiar with the dynamics of change and manage their consequences (Birasnav, 2014).

The leader must develop a strategy to control each of the forces. The strategy must be aimed either at strengthening the forces of the movement, weakening the forces of resistance, or both (Shahhosseini et al., 2013). Drivers of change can arise both outside and inside the organization. External factors include a changing political environment or a strategy for developing health care and medical science, a reduction in budget funding, changes in local governance, changes in the state of health of the population, and the introduction of new legislation. Inside an organization, the movement for change may be the result of management. Or it may arise spontaneously or be based on the initiative from lower-level employees (Yasin Ghadi et al., 2013). Change may be imitated by employees based on factors such as dissatisfaction with pay, poor working conditions, unstable funding, quality of the institution, and change of leadership (Ugwu et al., 2016). A manager must consider all variables and learn to manage resistance. In this way, a leader must consider change as a natural process, show respect to his or her opponents, and ideally create a rational approach that can be accepted by the opposition.

Since Becker's 1974 introduction of the theory of social interaction, there has been several additions to the theoretical framework through peer-reviewed research. Ben-Sira (1976) was one of the first authors to explore the theory within the vein of professional behavior and client satisfaction. He interviewed

1,892 adults to assess how their interactions with professionals led to their satisfaction with the experience. Participants remarked that the interactions between the professionals of each industry were critical toward their satisfaction and continued willingness to visit the same business. Ben-Sira's foundational work was critical to assessing how interactions between laypeople and professionals were impactful toward a business.

However, most applicable to this study is Rogoff's 1990 investigation of how social interactions influence the cognitive development between apprentices and their supervisors. Rogoff argued that the interactions between supervisors and their apprentices (e.g., subordinates) are not mutually distinct and must be assessed as a series of transmutable social interactions that have varied impacts on their mutual work performance.

During the twenty-first century, researchers such as Hartnell, Kinicki, and Lambert (2016) have assessed social interaction theory as a framework for the interactions between employees, supervisors, and CEOs. These studies are critical to the understanding of how the relationship of leadership styles is formed by the social interactions between leaders and their followers, and vice versa. In this vein, researchers Mencl and Wefald (2016) argued that the personality and social traits of a leader are vital to the social interactions they have with their subordinates and colleagues. Thus, according to Mencl and Wefald, within the framework of social interaction theory, an efficient leader must have suitable qualities, capabilities, skills, and knowledge to guide public health or medical science organization to success.

Social interaction theory creates a strong theoretical methodology as it provides a framework for analysis, an efficient method for field development, and a clear explanation about the views of participants (Ramos, 2017). Social interaction theory was appropriate for developing the problem of addressing the use of transformational and transactional leadership within mental health care counselors and managers because it allows for an exploration of how effective leadership guides their followers to successful social interactions with their subordinates. Social interaction theory was appropriate for developing the purpose of transformational and transactional leadership within mental health-care counselors and managers because it frames the exploration of how transformational and transactional leadership work through social interactions to lead to positive outcomes between counselors and managers. Social interaction theory was appropriate for developing research questions regarding the use of transformational and transactional leadership style from the perspective of counselors and managers to lead to positive work outcomes and positive relationships because the theory is based on the conceptualization of social interactions as a methodology to create positive outcomes within the workplace.

Thus the theory of social interaction will be used within this study to frame the exploration of literature and the results from this study. In particular, the theory of social interaction will frame the understanding of the usage of transformational and transactional leadership to create impactful relationships between mental health counselors and their mental health managers. Ideally, the use of this theory will expand the current understanding of how social interaction theory is applicable to the understanding of transformational and transactional leadership within the mental health care field. The theory of social interaction was designed to explain social interactions through thoughts and practices that coincide with the following research questions.

Review of the Literature

This section begins with the general topic of defining transactional and transformational leadership. First, an overview of leadership styles and traits within current and past academic research is provided. Next, a subsection is designated to discuss the current understanding of leadership traits in academic literature. A following subsection details the academic literature related to an individual associating as a leader through his or her actions and personality.

A critical analysis of the characteristics of leading in a specific situation follows. A subsection then explores leadership and goal-setting characteristics within a team. Following subsections discuss vision, direction, establishing a purpose, communicability, motivation and inspiration, organization, support, confidence, and ensuring productivity. The next section discusses the broad definitions of transformational and transactional leadership. This section includes a subsection discussing the historical context of transformational and transactional leadership. The following section provides a review of transactional leadership style.

A new section discusses the application of transactional and transformational leadership styles in business, health care, and mental health care fields. Finally, a summary is presented to assess the gaps in the reviewed literature and emphasize the importance of the reviewed literature to the purpose of this study.

General Definitions of Leadership Skills and Traits

This section establishes general definitions of leadership and provides current academic perceptions toward common leadership traits and skills. These studies do not directly address leadership styles for mental health and substance abuse counselors. However, they provide foundational knowledge concerning the use of leadership styles to promote and motivate employee career advancement. Understanding the foundational definitions of leadership skills and traits is key to assessing the usefulness of transformational or transactional leadership styles to mental health managers. Definitions of transformational and transactional leadership are briefly reviewed in this section but will be discussed in depth in following sections.

Researchers have frequently asked how leaders develop their successful skills. Many have asked if an individual is innately born with leadership qualities or if these skills are developed via experience. For instance, Karagianni and Montgomery (2017) assessed the development of leadership skills in young adults. The authors performed a critical analysis of leadership studies in the past ten years to learn how young adults develop leadership skills. They argued that it was key to understand how young adults develop leadership in order to assess how leadership skills develop throughout a person's lifetime. The authors reviewed a total of 413 articles and found that only nine articles used standardized methods of analysis when assessing young adults. The authors noted that leadership skills are seemingly developed through educational programs at a young age but are nurtured through continued leadership activities in adulthood. The majority of current studies posit that leadership is developed through experience (Byrne, Crossan, & Seijts, 2018; Karagianni & Montgomery, 2017; Porthouse, 2018; Sousa & Rocha, 2019).

Some researchers noted that leadership may be more natural for some individuals, but the potential for leadership does not guarantee that a person will become a true leader in life (Cranny-Francis et al., 2017; Ghani et al., 2018; Giltinane, 2013). For example, Shamir and Eilam (2005) conducted a thorough review of literature pertaining to the development of literature and found that successful leaders are typically self-reliant and familiar with their innate leading abilities. However, they noted that leadership is still developed through vital lived experiences, which shape their modes of leadership. The authors' study, which was a literature review based on synthesizing modern conceptualizations of leadership, is a foundational study regarding the common perceptions of leadership development in academic literature. These researchers indicated that the current conceptualizations of leadership development are centered around lived experiences and expertise that guide leaders to successfully lead, inspire, and motivate their teams (Karagianni & Montgomery, 2017; Shamir & Eilam, 2005; Sousa & Rocha, 2019).

Multiple researchers (Giltinane, 2013; Hamstra et al., 2014; Hargett et al., 2017) have argued that leadership definitions are broad and ambiguous. Traditional definitions of a leader include two important features: first, the individual is a self-starter, and second, the person can lead people (Allio, 2016; Ford, Harding, & Gilmore, 2017). However, the development of unique leadership styles is more frequently researched than developments of a standardized definition of a leader (Allio, 2016; Ford et al., 2017). Allio posited that leadership can be learned but cannot be taught. Allio did not perform an analysis but did provide a peer-reviewed synthesis of teaching and learning leadership via his personal experience within corporate industries. He argued that the development of leadership skills should be nurtured through multiple stages and lived experiences. The author further argued that leaders can learn leadership by three main tenets: associating as a leader, educating oneself on skills and traits of leadership, and engaging in leadership activities. Allio's research is a useful examination of how an individual can learn or develop leadership skills and traits through experience and practice.

Despite the three tenets suggested by Allio, the definition of the traits of a leader are not standardized across literature (Butler, 2002). However, there are several recurring themes concerning leadership traits within academic discourse. These themes are varied throughout literature, but the most prominent ones are discussed in the following subsections by reviewing associated academic research that has explored the applicability of each skill to leadership settings. These themes are reviewed as they commonly appear in literature regarding transformational and transactional leadership in business, health care, and mental health care studies. Thus it is important to be familiar with the usage of these traits in academic literature.

Leadership Traits

Seminal literature regarding leadership traits was first discussed in 1991 by Kirkpatick and Locke. The authors noted that leadership traits had been thoroughly debated within academic literature. According to the authors at the time of the publication, commonly cited leadership characteristics were drive, motivation, ambition, energy, and tenacity. Kirkpatick and Locke performed a literature synthesis, discussed each leadership trait, and emphasized why each trait was vital to the success and development of leaders. The authors emphasized the importance of examining and defining leadership traits for leadership studies.

Kirkpatick and Locke's seminal literature provided a foundation of defined leadership skills that studies continued to use for analysis. However, it is important to consider that these skills were only assessed through critical analysis of literature, not tested via quantitative or qualitative methodology.

Conversely, recent literature has slightly shifted away from specific standardized definitions of leadership, such as those employed in the study by Kirkpatick and Locke. For example, Mendoza, Orea-Amador, and Kendall (2016) investigated the leadership traits within a participant group of leaders to assess how leadership traits could possibly evolve with time and experience. The authors conducted an analysis of four sophomore undergraduate students who were leading high school students through a university program. Participants were allowed to guide their teams using any method that best fit their needs. An observer was assigned to monitor the leadership. Participants were also assigned leadership surveys to assess their perceptions of their leadership skills. Mendoza et al. found that participants initially described their leadership styles and general traits as being role models, delegators, and motivators, as well as to encourage participation within their teams. However, by the end of the program, participants described their leadership styles and traits as guided by inspiring their teams, focusing on confidence within their teams, and communicating effectively (Mendoza et al., 2016). The authors argued that their study indicates that the traits by which a leader is defined may be self-assessed and will ultimately change with experience and personal growth.

In sum, the original field of leadership focused on defining specific traits of a leader (Kirkpatick & Locke, 1991). However, the findings of Mendoza et al. (2016) emphasized the changing nature of leadership traits. Notably, the latter's study is useful for the current study as it considered how leadership skills and styles range between each individual, field, and team. As such, a standardized definition of a leader or specific traits a leader should obtain is not present in modern academic literature. However, the authors reviewed in this section noted that a leader can develop through lived experiences and leadership practice (Kirkpatrick & Locke, 1991; Mendoza et al., 2016). Furthermore, these studies indicated that the traits of a leader are variable by each individual and may change over a lifetime (Mendoza et al., 2016).

Yet there are recurring themes present in current literature regarding the specific traits and qualities of being effective leaders. The following qualities are leadership skills listed within the available academic literature. All of these may not be part of a leader's personality, but leaders ideally possess a few of these traits (Allio, 2016).

Associating as a Leader

Typically, leaders must first have associated as leaders to advance their careers in leadership (Jacobs & Kushnar, 2016). At this point, it is important to an individual to accept him- or herself and be able to motivate and discipline him- or herself and to set goals and achieve them (Cranny-Francis et al., 2017). Higgs and Duleqicz (2016) provided a thorough review of the characteristics of leadership. They also discussed the development of leadership skills. The authors argued that a key element in leadership traits is to visualize oneself as a leader. This may be an innate draw to leadership or a characteristic developed over time. In fact, authors such as Warren Bennis dedicated their lives to the academic research of how to be a leader (Cummings, 2017). However, contemporary literature and academic research are currently aimed at leadership styles, methods, and practices for industry-specific leaders. Yet associating as a leader is a crucial step in leading a team and building confidence in one's leadership styles (Higgs & Duleqicz, 2016).

Leading in a Situation

The next vital characteristic noted in academic literature is to be a leader in crucial situations. This is the first level of leadership. It is often considered leadership at the micro-level (Cranny-Francis et al., 2017). At this point, a person will ideally take responsibility for the actions of the entire group, regardless of the situation. This type of leadership is often the first seen among children in youth or sports groups, when one friend takes charge of a situation (Cranny-Francis et al. 2017). Susan Schwartz (2017) noted that a leader is most often defined by his or her choices in critical situations. Rosenbach (2018) noted that taking charge or leading a situation can identify a leader to a team or an employee. Rosenbach, who developed a recent book on leadership styles and traits, noted that leading in a situation and taking responsibility for the outcome of a situation is a crucial step in identifying as a leader. Thus, the decisions, actions, attitudes, and behaviors of a leader are vital reflections of a skilled or an unskilled leader in an organization. The next trait discussed is the ability for an individual to lead a team.

Leading a Team

This is the second level; leadership skills are already advancing at this point. Such leadership implies the solution of more important and complex goals. As a rule, leadership qualities begin to manifest precisely at this level between the ages of twenty to thirty, when a person takes a job (Cranny-Francis et al., 2017; Nawaz & Khan, 2016). Multiple researchers have investigated the connection between leadership and the ability to lead a team. Nawaz and Khan conducted a literature synthesis of leadership traits and argued that the ability for a leader to inspire, motivate, and encourage a team is vital to effective leadership. Thus, according to Nawaz and Khan, a leader must be able to lead a team and encourage team members to complete a common goal.

Goal Setting

This is the third level, leadership at the macro level. A person has an ambitious goal in life and leads a team to achieve these goals. Successful leadership at this level requires the development of certain leadership qualities (Cranny-Francis et al., 2017). Multiple academic resources exist to discuss the methods used to lead a team effectively (Archibald & Archibald, 2016; Watkins, 2016). However, many current leadership studies are focused on specific industries, methods, practices, and leadership styles (Alban-Metcalfe, 2018). In sum, it can be considered crucial to know how to lead a team as a manager. However, the methods used should be investigated according to the industry at hand (Cranny-Francis et al., 2017).

Vision

Leaders must have vision to create or reform a goal. According to Hamstra et al. (2014), vision allows for the creation of a new image, guides future goals, and helps provide perspective to current situations. Vision allows a leader to focus on a specific goal. Also, the ability to create a vision will help leaders unite and inspire people, arousing their desire to become followers.

Unlike a visionary or fantasy leader, a visionary leader constantly asks one very important question.

Direction

Direction allows the leader to formulate goals and vision into tangible results (Afsar & Umrani, 2019). This leadership skill allows a person to clearly see the goal, not just distant perspectives. When the result of an activity is formulated, the goal becomes clear and understandable. Direction allows a leader to set a path for the team to move toward the aforementioned goal (with an impassioned approach.

Establishing Purpose

According to Bonsu and Twum-Danso (2018), having a specific purpose is key to allowing leaders to face difficulties, persevere, find solutions to the problem, and move on. Leaders with a solidified purpose are able to work through challenges such as lack of resources. It is important not to confuse dedication with stubbornness and obstinacy. To develop perseverance, it is important to remember that there are no defeats, only feedback that helps you gain experience and draw the necessary conclusions on the way to achieving the goal (Birasnav, 2014).

Communicability

In today's world, the value of this leadership quality is very high. Being communicative is important not only as a leader but also in any other situations. Afsar et al. (2017) noted that the ability to communicate effectively is the key to success. Antonakis and Day (2017) argued that communicability is the ability to quickly establish contacts, to have an interlocutor, to listen, and the ability to ask questions and receive information. Sociability will allow you to create the right connections at the right time to achieve the goal more effectively. In today's world, this is called networking.

Motivating and Inspiring

The ability to motivate is to create an impulse of action that stimulates both oneself and others (Bonsu & Twum-Danso, 2018). There are usually two methods of motivation: from fear or love, or from minus or plus. It is necessary to apply different motivational techniques depending on the situation (Bass & Avolio, 1995; Bealer & Bhanugopan, 2014; Bonsu & Twum-Danso, 2018). Inspiration has also been noted as a form of motivation. It is more of a long-term motivational technique versus a short pulse of motivation (Attar et al., 2019).

Organization

Antonakis and House (2014) noted that it is very important for a leader to assemble and organize a team of first-class professionals. This includes those possessing such qualities as planning, documenting, and delegating. The entire team should work closely with a leader to reach the common goal. Typically, this is facilitated by group work, which is dependent on the total effort of the group. This brings together team members and allows a leader to cope more effectively with the tasks at hand.

Support

This leadership quality as a creator and team member includes the ability to support like-minded people and followers in difficult situations. People will support a leader who cares not only about his or her interests but also about them. Without this quality, it will be difficult for the leader to maintain authority. Going toward a goal is not only a challenge, it is also a strong relationship (Dai et al., 2013).

Confidence

Confidence is a state of mind connected with reliability (Birasnav, 2014). Birasnav's analysis of leadership literature noted that when individuals feel they can rely on a leader, they are more likely to trust and follow that leader. A confident person can be identified by body posture: straightened shoulders, slender posture, even breathing, low and distinct speech patterns, and looking at the other person.

Ensuring Productivity

Research conducted by Fischer (2016), Gabel (2013), and Giltinane (2013) noted that a leader must be active in all respects. The leader attempts to walk half a step ahead of time. He or she needs to have the latest information and be at the center of the event flow in order to act first. In the fast-paced world, a delay in productivity can indicate financial loss (Fischer, 2016; Gabel, 2013; Giltinane, 2013). It is important for goals to be set in action but also to encourage the continued movement of a plan.

Leadership Definitions of Transformational and Transactional Leadership

This section provides a historical context of transformational and transactional leadership. This review synthesizes the current understanding of transformational and transactional leadership. It provides foundational information regarding the methodologies that transactional and transformational leadership employ. It is vital to understand these basic tenets for future explorations of transformational and transactional leadership of mental health managers.

Following this section is a review of how these two leadership styles have been employed in business and health care fields. Furthermore, the use of transformational leadership has multiple advantages and disadvantages. This section discusses the definition of transformational leadership and explores previous studies who have used transformational leadership.

Historical Context of Transformational Leadership

In 1978, Burns defined transformational leadership. Burns's seminal publication noted that transformational and transactional leadership were two distinct concepts (McClesky, 2014). Burns (1978) formally defined transformational leadership as, "one [leader] who raises the followers' level of consciousness about the importance and value of desired outcomes and the methods of reaching those outcomes" (p. 141). He further emphasized that an organization should have a central goal that can unite leaders and employees (Stewart, 2006). It is important to note that during the time of Burns's publication, a central theory of leadership was not fully formed (Stewart, 2006). Thus, Burns's development of transformational leadership was a key moment in the field of leadership studies.

Transformational leadership later took on the value of a method of acknowledging the individual needs of employees to achieve organizational needs (McClesky, 2014). According to McClesky, on the creation of this methodology, transformational leadership was first explored as a method to improve the methodologies of business CEOs. Fields such as health care, military organizations, and entrepreneurs have since used transformational leadership to improve their leaders. Today, transformational leadership is used by multiple industries for meeting the needs of employees and organizations. The method of using transformational leadership often varies by each leader and organization, but the tenets of transformational leadership are based on the findings of Burns (1978), Bass (1986), and (McClesky, 2014). In 1985, the theory of transformational leadership was altered by Bass, who argued that transformational leaders should focus on four central tenets. These tenets are explored in depth in the following subsection.

Tenets of Transformational Leadership

It is important to review the tenets of transformational leadership to provide a knowledge base for examining the use of transformational leadership in the health care and mental health fields. For Bass (1986), the main characteristics of transformational leadership are: leadership by example, vision-inspired motivation, intellectual development, and individualized guidance. These tenets are visible within the research conducted by recent researchers.

According to research conducted by researchers Hamstra, Yperen, Wisse, and Sassenberge (2014), Shahhosseini and Silong

(2013), and Smith (2015), the primary reason transformational leadership works is the premise that leaders should use their own examples as motivators for the behavior of team members. Hamstra et al. investigated the methods of a transactional and transformational leader. The authors surveyed 120 leaders in the Netherlands identified with transformational and transactional leadership styles. The participants noted that they utilized these styles to help their employees meet organizational goals, which overall would ideally lead to a better organization. Hamstra et al. then employed a statistical analysis to assess if transformational and/or transactional leadership style was positively related to employee goal achievement. The authors' statistical analysis indicated that the use of transformational and transactional leadership styles was positively correlated with employee goal achievement. They also noted that their analysis indicates that these two leadership styles are key to motivating team members to achieving the desired goals or tasks of an organization.

Similarly, Shahhoseini and Silong (2015) investigated the connection of transactional and transformational leadership to guide employees to increase their job performance within an organization. The authors further argued that the emotional intelligence of a leader will lead employees to increased job performance. To test their hypotheses, the authors surveyed 192 managers in public and private banking sectors. Survey modes included an emotional intelligence test, a multifactor leadership survey, and a job performance survey. Results were qualitatively analyzed to assess if participants impacted employees with their use of emotional intelligence through transformational and transactional leadership styles. Shahhoseini and Silong found that participant leaders were able to engage employees more effectively via their use of emotional intelligence, which ultimately led employees to increase their performances. The authors argued that their findings agreed with previous studies that posited transformation and transactional leadership styles are key in utilizing emotional intelligence to promote job performance.

A similar study to those of Shahhoseini and Siolng (2015) and Hamstra et al. (2014) was conducted by Smith in 2015 to assess the use of transformational and transactional leadership to aid leaders within academic health care fields. Smith, however, did not employ a participant driven study but provided a synthesis of the use of transformational and transactional leadership to guide health care leaders to lead their employees to improve their job performance. Smith, through his critical analysis, argued that behavior sciences have emphasized that transactional and transformation leadership allow a leader to connect with his or her employees and guide them to a more effective team. Smith's analysis, though peer-reviewed, was not based on participant or observational data, but the author's study is useful for this analysis as it discussed the use of transformational and transactional leadership styles to be effective in health care fields.

These studies ultimately indicate that the use of transformational and transactional leadership styles is useful for motivating employees via emotional intelligence to increase job performance and meet organizational goals.

Summary of Transformational Leadership

For Bass, the main characteristics of transformational leadership are leadership—for example, vision-inspired motivation, intellectual development, and individualized guidance. According to research conducted by different researchers, the primary reason transformational leadership works is due to the premise that leaders should use their own examples as motivators for the behavior of team members (Hamstra et al., 2014; Shahhosseini et al., 2013; Smith, 2015). The intellectual development of subordinates through shared decision-making and incentive innovation are key components of the transformational leadership structure. When processes are considered ineffective in the pursuit of vision, the transformational leader encourages subordinates to seek innovative ideas and make decisions without the fear of criticism (Odumeru & Ogbonna, 2013). So instead of stating that a certain approach is wrong, the transformational leader helps subordinates see different ways of overcoming problems and challenges.

The ultimate characteristic of transformational leadership is individualized guidance. The leader celebrates the team effort but seeks to understand and meet the individual needs of subordinates. Therefore, the leader must be able to recognize the personal needs and desires of the subordinates (Kim & Shin, 2017). Therefore, transformational leadership aims to find ways to meet individual needs and align them with the vision and purpose of the team.

The first clear advantage of transformational leadership is engraved in its own name: transformation. According to Prasad and Junni (2016), the structure of transformational leadership aims to create change and innovation in organizations through a clear and shared vision about the future. In this way, the transformational leadership approach helps the organization to precisely define its objectives and make it easier for subordinates to commit.

The structure of transformational leadership also tends to strike a balance between short- and long-term goals. As the transformational leader's first step is to set meaningful long-term goals and then set achievable short-term goals (Rawung et al., 2015).

In addition to the above advantages, transformational leadership increases collaboration rather than competition within the team. By creating a shared vision for the team, the transformational leader inspires all team members to work together to achieve this vision. In this way, the transformational model increases cooperation among subordinates, which in turn improves outcomes and implements changes within the organization (Smith, 2015).

Transactional Leadership Style

The transactional model is based on two basic theoretical principles. First, each individual's behavior, choices, and ways of acting are guided by his or her life goals. Each individual, therefore, uses a rational approach that will allow him or her to reach the goal (McCleskey, 2014).

Next is positive behaviors. Positive behaviors help individuals to achieve their goals more quickly and effectively. This is typically associated with a positive reward if goals are met and maintained. However, if goals are abandoned, negative consequences follow (Van Knippenberg & Sitkin, 2013).

According to these principles, the group's primary objective is to obey the leader's instructions and commands of the leader—which must be as clear and precise as possible—not the global goal to which the leader aims. This is where the primary difference lies between this transactional leadership model and other types of leadership styles (Yahaya & Ebrahim, 2016). For example, in the relational or emotional model, work is carried out with an aim to share and complete a final goal. Conversely, in transactional leadership every member of the group is only required to carry out his or her task, without being able to have a more global perspective (Vito et al., 2014).

It is important to note that current researchers examine the effectiveness of transactional leadership when combined with transformational leadership. However, some studies have noted that transactional leadership can be useful when employed alone. For example, Chaudhry and Javed (2012) investigated the use of transactional leadership to motivate employees. The authors investigated their hypotheses by surveying 278 participants. Survey results were statically analyzed to understand if motivation was positively correlated with transactional leadership style. Chaudhry and Javed found that transactional leadership was more successful among participants in motivating their employees. The authors argued that transactional leadership may be a useful technique for leaders whose aim is to motivate employees.

However, research such as that of Chaudhry and Javed is rare in more recent literature. Current literature assesses the use of transactional and transformational leadership together to motivate, inspire, and encourage employees to meet organizational goals.

Summary of Transactional Leadership Characteristics

Transactional leadership is a leadership model described by the psychology of work that places as the foundation of its operation the leader's ability to improve employee performance on a reward-punishment basis (Rawung et al., 2015). This type of leadership is based on a sort of negotiation between the leader, who has the power to bestow the prize, and the collaborators, who must try to perform the tasks assigned to them if they want to get the rewards and avoid the punishments (McCleskey, 2014; Odumeru & Ogbonna, 2013; Podsakoff et al., 1990). However, studies within the past five years indicate that transformation and transactional leadership used together are the most effective response toward organizational goals.

Transformational and Transactional Leadership in Business

In this section, we explore the applications of transformational and transactional leadership in the business field, the sector most likely to use these leadership styles. Several researchers have addressed the use of leadership styles in this field (e.g., Birasnav, 2014; Esty & Bell, 2018; Ghani et al., 2018; Hamstra et al., 2014; Sheshi & Kercini, 2017). These authors are reviewed and critically examined in the following sections.

Moorman and Fetter (1990) similarly used the Multifactor Leadership Questionnaire (MLQ), which included a five-point Likert scale that ranged from 1, strongly disagree, to 5, strongly agree. Moorman and Fetter found the questionnaire was adequate for qualitative examinations of leadership studies. However, limitations were noted regarding the use of the scale. For example, not all respondents may have given a completely honest opinion due to the semi-personal nature of some of the questions. Also, due to multicultural nature of the respondents, all the cultural dimensions might not have been covered in the questions.

Moorman and Fetter's 1990 study, though dated, is noted here as the studies discussed in this section frequently use these scales to assess leadership effectiveness within organizations. Not all studies reviewed use these methodologies, but it should be noted that the use of questionnaires and Likert scales are not without limitations.

Sheshi and Kercini (2017) conducted research on the role of participative leadership and transformational and transactional leadership in business. The researchers gathered data from one hundred participants on a questionnaire. Sheshi and Kercini aimed to determine the performance of small and medium businesses via a descriptive quantitative exploration. The authors further assessed the efficiency of three business models (transactional, transformational, and democratic/participative leadership) that were then tested for impact differences using an ANOVA test. The authors found that out of three styles of leadership, two leadership styles positively impacted the performance of business activities. Transactional and democratic/participative leadership methods proved to have positive impacts on business organizations. The authors argued that the use of these models best fit organizational values and connected employees to these goals. Sheshi and Kercini argued that although future research is needed, their study found valuable quantifiable information regarding the effectiveness of variable models. The authors' study indicated that transactional and democratic/participative leadership are effective as they connect the beliefs of employees with organizational goals.

Similar research has been conducted to investigate the effectiveness of various leadership models. Fadhilah et al. (2018) investigated the correlation among transformational and transactional styles of female leadership and employee associations. The authors analyzed data based on responses from 113 participants. The authors also attempted to examine previous academic assertions that employees prefer male leadership. The researchers used SPSS quantitative software to evaluate the findings. Researcher findings indicated a positive association between both female transformational and transactional leadership styles and employee engagement. The limitations were that employees who were participants could not be located due to the lack of resources. Fadhilah et al. successfully illustrated that female leadership is desirable over male leadership. Sheshi and Kercini (2017) framed their research on the characteristics of the transformational leadership style and transactional leadership style. Fadhilah et al. added gender to the transformational leadership style and transactional leadership style in business world. The addition of gender as a variable within leadership studies contributed to the overall diversity of leadership studies.

One similar example of gender exploration is a study completed by Kim and Shin (2017). They examined the effectiveness of transformational leadership on employee empowerment. The authors employed a quantitative descriptive design using a five-point Likert scale survey. A total of 339 participants were included in the study. The respondents filled out questionnaires using the traditional paper-pencil method. Kim and Shin did not find significant gender differences on psychological empowerment; however, male employees were more positively impacted by transformational leadership. Kim and Shin's study was effective in conveying that psychological power was not gender-related. However, the authors did not significantly explore the leadership qualities that were most effective for leaders, regardless of gender. Yet the Kim and Shin study is one of the few examinations of gender within leadership studies.

Other studies have focused on the impact of leadership within entrepreneurial fields. Afsar et al. (2017) investigated transformational leadership, transactional leadership, and employees' entrepreneurial behavior. They gathered data from questionnaires given to 557 employees and their managers. The authors found that both leadership styles impacted employees differently and altered their entrepreneurial behaviors. The authors utilized a framework based on psychological empowerment, which would ideally utilize transformational and transactional leadership to inspire employees. Asfar et al. found employees tended to perform more efficiently when they had leaders who supported their emotional tendencies. The authors' study indicated the usefulness of transformational and transactional leadership style toward business and entrepreneurial models. The study's authors recommended that the use of a longitudinal study could be useful in exploring the causality and association among psychological behaviors and transactional and transformational leadership.

Other authors have examined the relationship between leadership styles and sharing knowledge across employees. Rawung, Wuryaningrat, and Elvinita (2015) conducted research within small businesses and assessed the use of transformational leadership and transactional leadership toward knowledge sharing. The authors' framework was founded on the attributes of leadership tactics. Transformational leadership tactics were comprised of motivational sources, inspirational sources, intellectual stimuli, and individual considerations. Transactional leadership tactics were comprised of management by exception and contingent rewards. The authors found that transformational leadership was more effective in creating associations between manager and employee. Their findings indicated that transformational leadership style can be an effective method for motivating employees. However, the authors' findings differ from the research of Sheshi and Kercini (2017), who found that transactional leadership was more successful.

Other authors have investigated the difference in leadership style effectiveness toward motivating employees and meeting organizational goals. Francis (2017) examined the impact of transformational leadership and transactional leadership styles on leaders in an administrative position. The authors employed a psychological test and the MLQ to assess the differences between leadership styles. The independent variable was transformational; the dependent variable was transactional. Francis's findings indicated a positive relationship with both leadership styles for administrative leaders. Francis noted that transactional leadership is most effective in business organizations, while a transformational leadership style is found to be more operative in long-duration business relationships. The results also showed a significant correlation between transformational and transactional leadership styles in effectively motivating and leading employees. Francis argued that the use of both leadership styles was effective for motivating employees and connecting them to organizational values. This study is one of the few to suggest that transformational and transactional leadership should be used in tandem to promote employee cooperation.

Taylor's (2017) research agreed with Francis's findings. Taylor evaluated transactional and transformational leadership methods between management and employees in the business world. The methodology was an online survey consisting of twenty-three questions. This research used a quantitative approach. Taylor showed that transformational leadership was successful in inculcating positive influence in followers. Taylor's findings supported the use of transactional and transformational leadership within private and public sectors for effective management of organizations.

Multiple experts have attempted to assess the use of transactional and transformational leadership in terms of a global economy. Zeb, Saeed, Rehman, Ullah, and Rabi (2015) studied performance in the public sector. Zeb et al. utilized the independent variable in their study. Transformational and transactional leadership methods were measured through an adopted version of the MLQ-5x/Short Form, developed by Avolio and Bass (1995). The authors found that both styles of leadership impact organizational goals within a global economy. Zeb et al. argued that both styles should be used to achieve effective results within the global economy.

However, not all authors agree with the findings of Zeb et al. (2015). For example, Bonsu and Twum-Danso (2018) explored leadership style in the global economy. Their study employed examples of the leadership characteristics by explaining how transformational and transactional leadership roles impact employees. Bonsu and Twum-Danso did not utilize a measurement instrument as Zeb et al. did in their 2015 leadership study. As such, Bonsu and Twum-Danso found that transformational leadership should be utilized with a cross-cultural leadership style to be most effective in a diverse global economy. The authors argued that their findings are centered toward a globalized economy, which requires methodologies tailored to the needs of multiple cultural backgrounds. However, the difference in Bonsu and Twum-Danso's methodologies, which differed from those used by Zeb et al., may explain differences in the study's findings toward transformational and transactional leadership. It should further be noted that Bonsu and Twum-Danso failed to provide qualitative questions to examine differences between leadership styles, thereby limiting the efficacy of their study.

Other studies have focused more specifically on the use of transformational leadership. Ugwu, Enwereuzor, and Orji (2016) examined the role of leadership between transformational leadership and employees in a small business. The authors investigated their hypotheses by exploring the roles of 170 factory workers and six supervisors. Ugwu et al. employed a hierarchical multiple regression model to assess the use of transformational leadership to empower trust between subordinates and supervisors. The authors found that transformational leadership was successful in motivating employees and ensuring that employees trusted their supervisors. The authors further noted that transformational leadership style was effective even if employees did not have significant bonds or relationships with their supervisors. The authors successfully examined the impact of transformational leadership within a large corporation to motivate and connect with employees.

Similarly, Olten, Bøllingtoft, Carneiro, and Borg (2018) examined the universality of transformational leadership. Olten et al. employed a quantitative descriptive methodology that surveyed 179 employees and 176 supervisors. Data was gathered by the use of the MLQ. The authors' framework was based on three items: transformational leadership, trust in leadership, and role in performance. For future research, the authors advised that culture should be taken into consideration when examining employee trust in leadership. This research may have a different outcome using a qualitative approach. However, the authors' research was useful in noting that while transformational leadership is useful, culture should be considered carefully in leadership methods.

Ahmad, Abbas, Latif, and Rasheed (2014) researched the universality of transformational leadership across native and immigrant employees within a telecommunication sector in

Pakistan. The authors completed a large-scale, quantitative, descriptive study across 2,836 native employees and 111 employees. The authors argued that employees are motivated by inspirational motivation, intellectual stimulation, individualized consideration, and idealized influence and behaviors of their peers. They found employee motivation is a key factor for participants. The study showed that employees are motivated by inspiration and intellectual stimulation. However, the degree to which these impacted participants was not explored due to the constraints of the study.

Ahmad et al. further stated that transformational leadership was useful in motivating employees and inspiring them based on individual needs. The authors' study was useful in assessing the use of transformational leadership style to motivate and inspire employees, but the study lacked a significant discussion of the applicability of their study to larger understandings of leadership within global economies.

Hamstra et al. (2014) sought to find the impact of transactional and transformational leadership on employee motivation and attitude. They also studied the resilience of transactional and transformational leadership. Hamstra et al. researched the ability to share leadership qualities between managers and employees. Each approach resulted in different findings. Previous researchers, such as Masa'deh et al. (2016), found that transactional leadership would lead to successful organizations. However, Hamstra et al. found that transformational leadership flexibility demands leadership that is both able to embrace change and operate within established structures until the need for a structural change arises. The findings of Hamstra et al. revealed that both transformational and transactional leadership styles have significant impact on job performance and, ultimately, on firm performance. The authors also argued that transactional leadership impacted knowledge-sharing, whereas transformational leadership did not (e.g., Masa'deh et al., 2016).

Summary of Business Leadership Research

Notably, within these examinations, the framework used to guide the exploration of transactional and transformational leadership style vary according to the researchers. Asfar et al. (2017) utilized a longitudinal study to assess the psychological impact of transformational and transactional leadership. Quantitative methodologies were employed by multiple authors to test the statistical differences in leadership impact on employees and organizational values (e.g., Fadhilah et al., 2018; Sheshi & Kercini, 2018). Some authors focused on gender, although gender explorations have been primarily dominated by male-centric ideologies of leadership (Fadhilah et al., 2018).

Studies by Fischer (2016) and Hargett et al. (2017) corroborated findings on several points, including that transformational and transactional leadership behaviors positively influence organizational innovation. In addition, the findings of the study conducted by Attar et al. (2019) revealed that transformational leadership was positively related to followers' endorsement of mastery goals. Finally, Hamstra et al. (2014) demonstrated that transactional leadership was positively related to followers' endorsement of performance goals. Although it keeps the motivation of the employees high, the limitation of this is that it is linked with reward and punishment, which denotes that if the motivation is removed, the motivation factor to work may also vanish sooner or later. However, the framework differed in each of the studies. Hamstra et al. used achievement goals; goal orientation; and motivation, transactional, and transformational leadership. Prasad et al. (2016) focused their framework around transformational and transactional leadership and organizational innovation.

This diverse approach did not result in different outcomes in the results that showed transformational leadership had a positive relationship between manager and employees (Hamstra et al., 2014). Studies conducted by Jensen et al. (2019) and by Bealer and Bhanugopan (2014) used quantitative approaches. However, there were different results concerning transactional and transformational leadership between public and private employees (Bonsu & Twum-Danso, 2018; Yahaya & Ebrahim, 2016; Zeb et al., 2015).

Vito et al. (2014) stated that existing conceptualizations and measures of transformational and transactional leadership have unclear theoretical bases, confound leadership and its effects, and are not necessarily suitable for public organizations. Although both studies used the MLQ, the results were not convergent due to sampling size and lack of purpose clarity. Similar studies in transactional and transformational leadership were conducted by Attar, Jami, and Kalfaoğlu (2019); Bennett (2018); and Jones and Jones (2017), in which the authors used the MLQ leadership questionnaire. Nonetheless, the purposes of the study among the authors do not converge. The purposes were different in that some sought to understand transactional and transformational leadership in cultural intelligence; others examined to what extent a relationship existed between transformational and transactional leadership attributes. Another study looked at the impact of corporate rank on the most profitable organizations and the examination of the correlation between leadership styles and the career success of women in nonprofit organizations.

Though business leadership studies are not directly related to mental health counseling, these studies did provide foundational information regarding the use of transactional and transformational leadership styles to share knowledge (e.g., Rawung et al., 2015) and promote psychological motivation among subordinates (Afsar et al., 2017). However, Francis (2017) and Taylor (2017) found that both leadership styles are effective for administrative purposes. Similarly, Van Wart (2013) argued that transformational leadership rarely interferes with transactional leadership.

Recent research regarding the effectiveness of a specific leadership style has been mixed (Bonsu & Twum-Danso, 2018; Zeb et al., 2018). Some researchers have indicated that transactional leadership style is the most effective for motivating (Sheshi & Kercini, 2017). Other researchers have found that transformational leadership is more useful for motivation (Ahmad et al., 2014; Rawung et al., 2015).

Current research indicates that leadership styles are best based on the specific organization and needs of leadership. Studies have focused on business industries but did not review the needs of health care and substance abuse managers. However, the findings of the use of transformational and transactional leadership styles are useful for the current understanding of the effectiveness of leadership styles to motivate, inspire, and connect employees with organizational goals.

Leadership Studies in Healthcare

In this book, the role of leaders in the history of health and medical science are not explored. Examining the historical role of health and medical sciences—such as illustrating its presentation of prominent personalities, features, characteristics, and contributions—would confine this review to collective characteristics reflective of individual practitioners and cannot be fully replicated by future scientists or a practitioner (Cranny-Francis et al., 2017). However, leadership within industries and the methods found to be applicable within the health care field are methods that future health care leaders can replicate within their organizations. Thus, the following section reviews the use of leadership within health care and discusses the implications of applying specific leadership styles to medical practices.

Leadership has been applied within health care for similar reasons as business organizations, such as motivating and engaging employees (Gellis, 2001). Gellis investigated the application of transformational and transactional leadership within health care–related fields. Similar to previous studies of transformational and transactional leadership, the authors utilized the MLQ survey to assess the usefulness of transformational and transactional leadership within the field. The authors analyzed 187 social workers who were employed in county hospitals and found that the use of transactional and transformational leadership was useful for social workers to connect with their subordinates. Gellis argued that using transformational and transactional leadership together was a positive method for inspiring employees and preventing employee burnout. The analysis provided by Gellis indicates that specific leadership styles of transformational and transactional are utilized within health care.

A similar study was conducted by Krepia, Katsaragakis, and Kaitelidou (2018), who examined the use of transformational leadership to motivate nursing teams in Greek hospitals. The authors conducted a thorough analysis of current literature pertaining to the use of transformational leadership within nursing-related industries. Krepia et al. provided foundational definitions of transformational leadership and synthesized all current uses of the leadership style in nursing-related studies. The authors noted that transformational leadership style has been effectively utilized in nursing fields to motivate, engage, and effectively communicate with nursing teams. They also found that the transformational leadership style has been proven to be a technique to incite positive changes in a nursing team and an associated organization. The authors' study was useful in synthesizing the current literature on transformational leadership in nursing. The most useful element of this study was recognizing the historical and modern use of transformational leadership style to effectively manage nursing teams in health care.

Similarly, Patel, Ashrafin, Uzoho, Nikiteas, Panzarasa, Sevdalis, Darzi, and Athanasiou (2018) argued that transformational leadership can be a useful technique in health care–related fields. To test this, the authors applied the MLQ to ninety medical leaders in the United Kingdom. Patel et al. (2018) attempted to assess the leadership behaviors of each of the surveyed faculty. The authors noted that the MLQ was ideal as it provides assessments of leadership behavior, motivation, and satisfaction based on participant responses. Overall, the authors found that, based on the participant answers to the MLQ, leaders who used transactional or transformational (or both) leadership styles were able to positively influence changes within their organizations. The authors argued that the use of transformational and transactional leadership style could tentatively be considered an effective style for health care based on their study. However, it should be noted that the authors did not provide, due to the nature of the study data, why or how these leadership styles impacted their subordinates.

Summary of Leadership Studies in Healthcare

There is currently a lack of literature regarding the use of specific leadership styles in the health care field. The studies reviewed in this section represent the few studies that assessed specific leadership styles with participant data. However, Gellis (2001) did employ a literature synthesis. Current studies in leadership are guided toward examining case studies, participant surveys, or synthesizing literature related to leadership within health care. Within this section, Gellis noted that a combination of transformational and transactional leadership styles can be useful within health care.

The other authors reviewed in this section concurred with Gellis concerning transformational and transactional leadership styles (Krepia et al., 2018; Patel et al., 2018). However, each study utilized different methodologies. Krepia et al. performed a synthesis of nursing leadership literature. Gellis (2001) conducted an analysis of social workers in county hospitals. Similarly, Patel et al. (2018) assessed medical leaders within the United Kingdom using an MLQ survey. Each study emphasized the need for a leader to unite a medical health care team. However, none of these studies provided examples of how transformational or transactional leadership served to positively impact leaders in medical health care.

Leadership Studies in Mental Healthcare Fields

Leadership studies in mental health are limited. All sources within the past five years were utilized, but due to a lack of literature regarding leadership in mental health care, some research is older. This section is also designed to connect leadership concerning mental health care with the purpose of this study.

Gabel (2012) investigated leadership within mental health care. The author argued that mental health care can place tremendous stress on employees and managers due to the emotional nature of their field. Gabel further noted that mental health care managers have the unique role of keeping employee morale high and preventing employees from becoming discouraged or emotionally burdened. As such, the author explored a single case study of a mental health care manager who oversaw multiple psychiatrists. The author explored the manager's use of leadership via the participants' lived experiences. Gabel noted that the participant emphasized the need for mental health care managers to empower, listen, and communicate with their employees to avoid demoralization. The managerial participant remarked that his job was based on understanding that his employees' unhappiness often stemmed from the patients and patient-related decisions they were required to make.

According to Gabel, the participant emphasized that he employed his clinical knowledge to empathize with employees and attempt to recognize signs of discontent within his team. He also encouraged his entire team to be supportive of each other. Gable argued that this case study is an example of the unique challenges that a mental health care manager faces. However, the author argued that effective leadership can motivate, engage, and prevent employee burnout.

This study serves as an example of how one mental health care manager utilized leadership skills to prevent employee burnout and increase employee morale within his team. The author's study is also an excellent example of the use of qualitative methodologies to explore the usefulness of leadership skills within mental health care managers.

Similar methodologies have been employed to explore leadership within psychiatry. One seminal source on leadership in psychiatry is *Leadership in Psychiatry* (Bhugra, Ruiz, & Gupta, 2013). The processes used by various leaders are discussed within the book as they apply specifically to the field of clinical psychiatry. The authors approach their book as a methodological handbook for leaders in psychiatry, but the book is not a peer-reviewed source.

However, a similar but peer-reviewed article was written by Heok in 2010. The author assessed the need for further understanding regarding the application of leadership within the field of psychiatry. Heok noted that a psychiatric manager is expected to have extensive clinical skills and be aware of the duties of his or her peers and subordinates. Heok did not perform an analysis for his article but did provide a concise review of the expectations of leadership in psychiatry.

The author noted that some conferences, workshops, and workplace improvement conferences have been conducted to provide psychiatric managers with additional skills. He argued that training a few efficient leaders in psychiatry will lead to improved teams, and these leaders will ideally impart their knowledge and expertise to other psychiatric leaders. Heok's study did not test the assumptions, but the author did provide a concise synthesis of the current methods for psychiatric leadership training. According to the author, current training of psychiatric managers is based on expertise, lived experiences, and learning from others. However, the author did not emphasize a specific leadership style, such as transformational or transactional leadership, that is used by psychiatric leaders.

Other studies have expressed qualitative approaches to assess how mental health teams should be effectively led. Singh (2000) noted that mental health teams are typically comprised of multiple experts, such as psychiatrists and counselors. These facilities are guided by mental health care managers. The author noted that team building is crucial within such facilities and ideally engages and motivates employees to support each other. Singh reviewed the basic tenets of team building and noted that there are various barriers that prevent mental health teams from being effective. The author argued that these include a lack of resources, a lack of understanding which services need to be provided to which patients, poor gatekeeping to discourage minor mental health issues from overburdening the team, differences in ideologies toward practices, burnout of the staff dealing with patients, and overall resistance to change from team members.

Singh argued that most of these issues could be effectively mitigated by a competent leader focused on building a cohesive mental health care team. According to the author, a leader is key to rallying a team around central goals that lead to the betterment of the organization. In sum, the author's article, though literature synthesis only, indicated that mental health care facilities are guided by effective leaders, and effective leadership may help to prevent common mental health employee issues, such as burnout. However, it should be noted that the author did not conduct an analysis, collect participant interviews, or provide a case study on which to base the argument of the piece. Furthermore, Singh did not suggest or review the use of specific leadership styles that could best address the needs of a mental health care team.

One study did address the use of a specific leadership style within the mental health care field. Corrigan, Diwan, Campion, and Rashid (2002) analyzed the use of transformational leadership to guide a mental health care team. The authors surveyed fifty-four mental health teams in a mental health hospital in the United States. A total of 620 employees made up those mental health care teams. The authors collected data from 236 mental health care leaders who were directly in charge of guiding the teams. The leaders included specialties ranging from psychiatry, charge nurses, to clinical managers. An MLQ and an organizational description questionnaire were provided to leaders. Employees were provided the same questionnaire, which had been altered to assess their perceptions of the mental health care leaders.

Corrigan et al. found that leaders who identified with transformational or self-reported to identify with transactional leadership reported that their teams were satisfied and efficient. The authors further noted that transformational leadership in particular had a positive correlation with having an effective team. Despite these findings, the authors did note that leaders and employees ranked leadership efficiency differently. For example, leaders rated themselves positively, but employees rated their leaders slightly lower. Corrigan et al. argued that this indicates employees and leaders within the sample viewed leadership through different lenses, which could impact team efficiency. This study is the singular example of the examination of transformational and transactional leadership in the mental health care field. The authors' study indicated that these leadership styles could be useful for mental health care leaders. However, it should be noted that the authors did not discuss how these leadership styles were used to positively impact their employees and mental health care teams.

Summary of Mental Healthcare and Transformational and Transactional Leadership

Studies regarding the use of transformational and transactional leadership are limited in academic literature. However, some studies have provided foundational understanding of the application of these styles to mental health care leaders. Within this section, Gable's (2012) single case study indicated that transformational and transactional leadership style was effective for leaders to prevent burnout and motivate employees. Similarly, Heok (2010) found the use of these styles was effective for imparting knowledge among psychiatric health care leaders. Singh (2000) found that the combined transformational and transactional leadership style can be used to prevent challenges that employee teams face within mental health care facilities. However, Singh's critical analysis was primarily based on literature readily available in academic databases. Corrigan et al. (2002) provided the most information in their exploration of mental health care leaders' utilization of leadership styles to motivate employees and lead them to similar goals.

In sum, information about the use of transformational and transactional leadership styles is lacking in academic literature. However, the studies within this subsection indicated that transformational and transactional leadership have been used effectively within psychiatric and mental health care facilities to motivate, engage, share knowledge, and lead employees toward similar organizational goals.

Summary of Literature Review

This study is designed to assess the use of transformational and transactional leadership styles for mental health and substance abuse managers. General leadership traits were noted in current academic literature to be a broad definition dependent on the leaders and the industry, and there is not a standardized definition of a leader or leadership traits (Butler, 2002). However, authors have noted that leaders utilize personality traits, lived experiences, and leadership experiences to guide their employees and teams to meet organizational goals (Kirkpatick & Locke, 1991; Mendoza et al., 2016).

Healthcare in the mental health fields lacks significant studies addressing the use of transformational and transactional leadership styles. Most studies address the mental health care field broadly. Studies addressing the use of leadership styles for mental health care managers are limited. However, the studies available did find that transformational and transactional leadership styles were able to raise employee morale, prevent burnout, and empower employees (Bhugra et al., 2013; Corrigan et al., 2002; Gable, 2012; Heok, 2010; Singh, 2000).

In sum, more research is needed to understand how mental health care managers are utilizing (if they are) the methods of transactional and transformational leadership. As most research on the subject is dated (pre-2015), more current literature is also needed to understand if transactional and transformational leadership styles can be applied to assist mental health care managers in leading their employees.

Transactional leadership style alone is designed for employees to address the prompts of their leaders. Transformational leadership, however, is designed to inspire employees to mimic their leaders and make positive impacts and decisions together (McClesky, 2014). The advantages of both styles have been more modernly combined and is often referred to as transformational and transactional leadership style (McClesky, 2014; Odumeru & Ogbonna, 2013). However, some industries and leaders still choose to use either transformational or transactional leadership style to accomplish industry-specific goals (McClesky, 2014).

As transformational and transactional leadership style is frequently used differently in different industries, this review assessed the use of the styles within business, health care, and mental health care industries. Business was utilized within this review as it provided a foundational understanding of the most common application of transformational and transactional leadership style within academic literature. Furthermore, studies related to the use of these two styles in health care and mental health care are limited, and reviewing the application of these leadership styles in business provided a mirror for how these styles could be applied in differing industries.

In most studies assessing leadership, the MLQ is commonly used to assess the leadership capabilities of managers and administration (Moorman & Fetter, 1990). Multiple authors employed the transformational and transactional leadership styles to assess leadership within business fields (Shashi & Kercini, 2017). Some studies employed quantitative analysis to indicate that the leadership styles were useful in connecting employees to larger organizational goals (Sheshi & Kercini, 2017). Other authors found those styles were able to empower female leaders to motivate and encourage communication within their organizations (Fadhilah et al., 2018; Kim & Shin, 2017). In fact, these leadership styles were shown to be effective for entrepreneurs to connect with other leaders and empower their teams (Asfar et al., 2017). Authors such as Rawung et al.

(2015), Francis (2017), and Taylor (2017) further emphasized the ability of transformational and transactional leadership to share knowledge across employees and motivate them toward shared goals.

Overall, in the business industry, transformational and transactional leadership have been effectively employed to share knowledge across employees, motivate, encourage, and inspire employees. These styles have been effective in connecting employees to organizational goals and increasing employee performance and satisfaction (Bonsu & Twum-Danso, 2018; Yahaya, & Ebrahim, 2016; Zeb et al., 2015). As such, the critical analysis of business leadership styles indicated that mental health care fields could possibly benefit from the use of these methodologies. For example, sharing knowledge, connecting, and engaging are all elements needed within any employee-driven industry (Asfar et al., 2017).

The final two sections of this review turned to the application of transformational and transactional leadership styles within health care and mental health care fields. Cranny-Francis (2017) noted that health care fields are complex and require leaders with expertise to understand the unique needs and emotional burdens of employees. As such, transformational and transactional leadership styles have been found to be a successful approach for connecting employees to leaders and preventing employee burnout (Gellis, 2001; Krepia et al., 2018; Pate et al., 2018). However, studies using specific leadership styles are limited within current academic literature. Yet the studies reviewed indicated that these leadership styles could motivate, connect employees to leaders, and prevent employee burnout (Gellis, 2001; Krepia et al., 2018; Pate et al., 2018).

CHAPTER 3

Research Method

Although there is significant research on leadership within the business setting (for example, Smith & Khojasteh, 2014), there is a gap in the literature regarding the leadership relationship between counselors and managers in the mental health field (Bowen & Moore, 2014). In the mental health field, the relationship between counselor and manager does not currently benefit from the findings regarding the relationship between the manager and the follower in leadership research in business (Hesler, 2018). The purpose of this qualitative research was to fill the gaps in research and better understand how transactional and transformational leadership impact the counselor and manager relationship in mental health counseling settings. This study investigated specifically if, how, and to what effect transformational and transactional leadership styles are used in the mental health field. This information may impact the overall effectiveness of both the counselor and the manager in their respective job duties.

This chapter presents the research methodology for this study. Overall, the study is an investigation into the transactional and transformational leadership strategies used in the New York Hope Center (pseudonym) and the New York Substance Abuse Facility (pseudonym) mental health counseling offices. The perspectives will come from both the counselors and the managers working in these facilities. The qualitative descriptive study includes interviews that will be transcribed and analyzed using thematic analysis.

The design for this study was qualitative descriptive. The analysis used thematic analysis. Interviews were conducted with voluntary participants for the purpose of answering the research questions of this study. Interviews were transcribed, coded, and analyzed for themes using NVivo coding software. Study participants consisted of ten counselors and ten managers employed at the New York Hope Center (pseudonym) and the New York Substance Abuse Facility (pseudonym), which are centers for addiction and mental health care.

In this chapter, research methodology and design are first discussed. Justification for the choice of qualitative methodology is reviewed in contrast to other possible methods. The choice of the population and sample are reviewed, and the details regarding these individuals are discussed. The data collection instrument is reviewed in this chapter. Study procedures are reviewed, which includes the methods used to request voluntary participants for this study. Following is a thorough discussion of the methods for data collection and analysis. Finally, the study's assumptions, limitations, delimitations, and ethical assurances are reviewed.

Research Methodology and Design

A qualitative descriptive methodology was used in this study. Qualitative research is the process of exploring a research problem by investigating the lived experiences of individuals within a populace. Qualitative research was used to assess concepts that include individual emotions, opinions, or information regarding perceptions of sociocultural phenomenon (Korstjens & Moser, 2018). This is typically accomplished through methods such as interviewing or observing cultural phenomena examined through a prolonged engagement, such as long interviews with participants in order to become familiar with their professional relationships with managers in a mental health and substance abuse setting (Silverman, 2018).

This study used a qualitative descriptive design. Qualitative descriptive design involves the exploration of textual data as a means to describe a specific phenomenon (Denzin & Lincoln, 2011). The textual data in qualitative descriptive design is explored by assessing recurring themes, patterns, words, and phrases that appear during the textual data (Nassaji, 2015). The exploration of the identified themes allows the researcher to describe a phenomenon based on the textual data. The assumption of the method is finding out what can be known (Denzin & Lincoln, 2011). Sandelowski (2000) explained that qualitative descriptive design goes beyond the literal description of the data in order to interpret findings.

The qualitative descriptive design was appropriate for developing the problem that despite significant research on leadership within the business setting (Smith & Khojasteh, 2014), there is a gap in the literature regarding the leadership relationship between counselors and managers in the mental health field (Bowen & Moore, 2014). A qualitative descriptive design allowed for the exploration of this gap through the textual evidence gathered during data collection and then thematically analyzed.

The qualitative descriptive design was appropriate for developing the study's purpose—the exploration of how transactional and transformational leadership styles impact the counselor and manager relationship in mental health counseling settings—because a thematic analysis design is ideal for exploring impact based on lived experiences and perceptions.

Finally, the qualitative descriptive design was appropriate for developing the research questions regarding how transformational and transactional managerial tactics produce positive relationships and work outcomes between the counselor and the manager. The use of thematic analysis garners information that can be used to answer these researcher questions based on participants' remarks from their experiences.

Alternative methods for studying this phenomenon included quantitative methods. For this study, qualitative research was chosen to answer these research questions. Quantitative research involves empirical investigations of observable issues, which are analyzed using statistics and answerable hypotheses (Tracy, 2019). This researcher explored the reported experiences of mental health care counselors and managers. The lived experiences of each interviewed participant are unique and, therefore, not ideal for numerical assessments (Mihas, 2019). Rather, a qualitative methodology is appropriate to exploring the lived experiences of mental health care counselors and managers who have direct experience with leadership. For this study, the lived experiences of each interviewed participant were unique and not suitable for numerical assessment (Mihas, 2019). The choice of a qualitative design permitted a thematic analysis that involved the immersion of data through transcription, coding, selection, and organization of themes (Glesne, 2016). Additionally, qualitative methodology is a reliable method frequently used to assess valuable patterns from lived experiences reported by interview participants (Glesne, 2016; Mihas, 2019; Stuckey, 2015).

Alternative qualitative methods include ethnography, narrative, and case study. The first alternative method explored was ethnography. Ethnographic studies are designed to explore cultural phenomenon by directly observing (e.g., participant observation) within a specific culture or individuals of a specific culture (Tracy, 2019). Ethnographic designs typically entail the ability to spend extended lengths of time observing and interacting with a community or group of individuals (Taylor, 2002). This study does not explore cultural aspects of leadership but instead investigates the lived experiences of individuals who have interacted with transformational and transactional leadership styles. As such, ethnographic methodology was not used for this study.

The second possible alternative to the current study design was a narrative approach. A narrative approach is used to explore the experiences of individuals based on how a phenomenon has impacted them or evolved during their lifetimes or time spent utilizing a technique (such as leadership) (Trahar, 2006). However, this study aimed to understand the use of leadership within a particular field. Though information is garnered from specific individuals, the design assesses the evolution of leadership through the narratives of one or more individuals and is not appropriate for this study as it would not allow for an exploration of leadership within the broad context of the mental health field.

The third alternative was a case study. A case study is typically employed to assess the development of a phenomenon at a particular organization (Tracy, 2019). Case studies may also be employed to make comparisons between multiple organizations, such as comparing leadership between one hospital and another hospital. For this study, the author is concerned with the utilization of transformational and transactional leadership for mental health care managers and counselors, which is understudied in the current literature. As such, a case study was not appropriate as the problem statement is not aimed toward the use of these leadership styles at specific organizations.

Population and Sample

The targeted population of this study was mental health counselors and managers in a northeastern state. Specific data regarding the demographic variables of mental health care counselors and managers is limited (Heisler, 2018). However, population data from national trend research indicated that 73 percent of counselors are female. Additionally, 70.6 percent of counselors are Caucasian, and 19.8 percent are African American. Asian counselors in the United States compose 2.9 percent of the counselor workforce. Job growth for the counseling degree is estimated to rise 17 percent by 2026 (Data USA, 2018). Mental health care managers and counselors are required to take specific licensure and complete higher-education degrees.

Mental health care managers are typically responsible for overseeing mental health care work within their associated facilities and for assuring that the treatment provided is suitable for the patients (Substance Abuse and Mental Health Services Administration [SAMHSA], 2019). Mental health care managers are also charged with managing and overseeing the staff below them within the facility. The number of individuals that each manager oversees varies according to the facility by which they are employed. Mental health care counselors also provide services directly to patients through education, resources, treatment, therapy, assessment, and diagnosis (American Mental Health Counselors Association [AMHCA], 2019).

Mental health counselors are licensed and specialize in specific regions of mental health care, such as substance abuse therapy (AMHCA, 2019). Counselors typically work for an organization with other mental health care counselors or psychiatrists and work underneath the supervision of a mental health care manager (AMHCA, 2019; Heisler, 2018).

This population was appropriate to address the problem as the individuals in the mental health care field have direct experience with managing and being managed by the use of various leadership tactics. For this study, transformational and transactional leadership styles have been thoroughly addressed in various industries (e.g., business, hospitals, and education). However, studies addressing the use of transformational and transactional leadership styles for mental health care managers and counselors are absent in the available academic literature.

The population is appropriate to carry out the purpose of this study, which is to assess if and how the use of transformational and transactional leadership is used within the mental health care field. This is because mental health care counselors and managers play crucial roles in providing guidance and rehabilitation to their patients in stressful environments. Thus, the population of counselors and managers is ideal for furthering the current understanding of leadership in the mental health care field and for ideally furthering policies and practices regarding leadership in this field.

The population is appropriate to answer the research questions, which discuss the use of transformational and transactional leadership styles by mental health care managers to produce positive work outcomes for mental health care counselors and positive relationships between mental health care counselors and managers. The population was adequate to answer these questions as in the mental health care field, managers and counselors have direct supervisor to subordinate relationships. Thus, the research questions were appropriate to addressing the lived experiences of counselors and managers in the mental health care field who have experience managing and being managed.

Yin (2014) and Fusch and Ness (2015) argued that qualitative sample size should include sufficient participants to garner information regarding the studied topic. This can include a minimum of five to ten participants; however, there is not a standardized specific number of participants for qualitative analyses. This sample consisted of ten counselors and ten managers employed at the New York Hope Center (pseudonym) and the New York Substance Abuse Facility (pseudonym), which are centers for addiction and mental health care. They were chosen because they have appropriate counselors and managers, and for convenience. At the mental health and substance abuse facility, employees work directly with each other. Saturation was achieved when no new themes were being included in interviews. If saturation was not reached by fifteen participants, more were recruited. However, this was not deemed necessary due to saturation reached during data collection.

The inclusion criteria for the selection of these participants included three things. First, their place of employment is at a local mental health facility. Second, they must have five years of experience in the field of mental health services. Third, all participants selected must have the Credentials Alcohol and Substance Abuse Counseling (CASC) certification, or a license in social work. Most counselors obtain a bachelor's degree specializing in psychology or social work. Demographics are limited for specific regions and counties. The sample of individuals for this study include mental health care counselors with the degree and licensure of MHC-LP. Similarly, mental health care managers also obtain the title of MHC-LP and have significant experience as a counselor and as a manager within mental health care facilities. These individuals also earn the CASC certificate, which enables them to work directly with addiction-focused populations.

The sample of mental health care counselors and managers within a substance abuse and mental health care facility is appropriate to address the problem—which is the lack of understanding of the use of transformational and transactional leadership within the mental health care field—because the individuals who work in such facilities experience significant emotional work stress due the nature of their field (Bowen & Moore, 2014). Research has indicated that the relationship between the counselor and manager impact the therapeutic services provided to patients (Clipa & Greciuc, 2018). Thus, the individuals within this sample will be able to provide direct responses regarding their lived experiences with their counselors and managers to assess the use of leadership styles within the mental health care field.

Provided feedback include how their lived leadership experiences have been used to produce positive work outcomes. Counselors and managers will be able to respond to how managerial tactics—transformational, transactional, or combined leadership styles—were able to produce positive work relationships between each other. Sample responses regarding their lived experiences will further the understanding of how leadership managerial tactics are used to produce positive work outcomes and work relationships.

Participants were recruited for this study by an invitational email (appendix F) requesting voluntary participation in this study. The email was to the human resources (HR) department or to the secretary in the office of the facility employing the counselors and managers, who emailed them to the potential participants. The email informed the participants of the purpose of this study, discussed the role of the researcher, and provided the HR and Institutional Review Board (IRB) approval letters. The email discussed that the study results could improve future manager relations with counselors. It also assured each participant that participation was completely voluntary, and his or her answers would remain confidential. It informed the participants they would receive a stipend in the form of an Amazon e-card in the amount of $10. Individuals who responded to the email were included in the study, and the in-person conference for the interview was scheduled in a meeting room at the local library.

Data Collection Instrument

The data collection instrument for this study was the interview protocol found in appendix C. The data for this study was collected via semi-structured interviews conducted by the author. These interviews included a set list of interview questions developed by the author. The questions were written and organized to answer the study's research questions. Participants discussed transactional leadership first, addressing the work output and relationships separately. Then they discussed transformational leadership. To increase the credibility of the study, participants were given the same definitions of transactional and transformational at the beginning of the questions.

Participants received different interview questions based on their status. For example, mental health care managers were asked questions regarding their leadership styles. Conversely, mental health counselors were asked questions regarding their perceptions of leadership from their relationships with their corresponding managers. These research questions can be found in appendix C. Interview questions were designed following the recommendations for semi-structured interviews by Rabionet (2011). The proposed interview questions were field-tested in phone interviews with a counselor. The pilot information was not included in the study, only with the dissertation chair. This process was completed before the IRB application for the purpose of ensuring study validity during the application process.

Study Procedures

Participants were requested to join the study by an email informing them of the purpose of the study and assuring them of their confidentiality and anonymity. The email indicated the study was approved by the IRB. The participant email list was gained by requesting email addresses from the HR office of mental health counselors and managers. HR was informed that the list was only going to be used to request participation. If no responses were received during the first email request, the author sent out a second email requesting participants, continuing until a sufficient number of participants were obtained (see "Population and Sample").

Each participant was required to answer the same set of interview questions (see appendix C). However, follow-up questions were used if necessary to explore and/or expand on topics participants mentioned within the study. Each interview was conducted over the phone to ensure participant confidentiality. All participants received an email before the meeting again informing them that their participation was confidential and anonymous. They were required to sign a formal agreement to participate. I sent this to the participants by email, and it was emailed back to me. During the interviews, I recorded the responses and took notes.

After the interviews were completed, they were transcribed using the online service REV for expediency. Member-checking followed the procedures suggested by Madill and Sullivan (2017), which included providing the transcripts to the participants after the interviews to ensure the accuracy of the transcription. During the transcription process, all participants were provided pseudonyms to protect their confidentiality and to provide confidentiality during the analysis. For instance, a mental health counselor was labeled (C1). Similarly, a mental health manager was labeled (M1). The number in the pseudonym indicated different participants (e.g., C1, C2, C3).

Data Collection and Analysis

Data for this study was collected by conducting semi-structured interviews with study participants. The interviews were recorded by the author using an audiotape device. The device was the application of GoogleVoice, which allowed the researcher to record the phone interviews.

After all interviews were finalized, the recorded interviews were transcribed. Transcribing the data is key for familiarizing oneself with the textual data and for becoming immersed with the text for thematic analysis (Bailey, 2008; Bengtsson, 2016). As mentioned previously, pseudonyms were assigned to protect the confidentiality of the participants. For example, the mental health care managers were assigned MM and mental health care counselors were assigned CC. Numerical values were assigned to each participant to indicate individual interviewees (e.g., MM1 and CC1). After this step, the author began thematic analysis using the coding software NVivo to categorize and organize the textual data.

NVivo coding software allowed the researcher to apply codes to the data electronically and then use tools for visualization and the organization tool to explore the themes identified by the researcher (Zamawe, 2015). The process of coding was useful for organizing the data and providing meaning to patterns, phrases, or ideologies expressed by the participants (Nolen, 2018). The author reviewed each transcribed interview to identify similarities or differences that occurred across the textual data (Castelberry & Nolen, 2018). NVivo was used to categorize and organize these identified patterns identified by the author. Patterns, phrases, words, or key sentences were coded in NVivo using nodes, which is essentially tagging that allow the author to highlight and organize patterns within the data (Castelberry & Nolen, 2008). They were labeled by the author according to the category that the phrase, word, or paragraph indicates. For example, if the term "leadership" frequently occurred, the researcher placed corresponding text into the node of "leadership." The researcher used several tools within

NVivo to explore the textual data. For example, relationships between participants were recorded by the researcher using the relationship nodes that indicate a connection between elements of text. Other tools within NVivo include the text search query, which involves searching for a key word (e.g., leadership) and identifying if this word occurred frequently or infrequently within the text (Castelberry & Nolen, 2018). This tool was used to explore elements of text that possibly indicated relationships or should be included in a node.

The method of thematic analysis was appropriate to answer the research questions of this study. The researcher followed Castelberry and Nolen's guidelines for the analysis. This is accomplished by gaining firsthand interviews with individuals who have direct involvement and expertise in mental health care management and counseling. The interview, transcription, coding, and interpretation involved in thematic analysis led to textual data that can be used to qualitatively explore the research questions for this study. The research questions were addressed by exploring the resultant themes from thematic analysis and how they relate to the research questions by demonstrating the textual data resulting from participant interviews.

The analysis was used to answer the research questions as the answers being analyzed were directly aligned with the research questions. Participants' answers about the impact transactional and transformational strategies have on their work outputs and relationships were organized according to the research questions were answered as given without any comments about the questions.

The problem is that it is unclear what transactional and transformational strategies were being used in the context of counseling, and the answers to the interview questions would enumerate what those strategies are. In addition, the answers provide information on whether each strategy is effective for improving work output and relationships.

The role of the researcher in this process is complex. It is important to note the researcher's bias and previous experience so that he can be aware of them and try not to let them influence his interpretation of the data. For example, this researcher is biased toward transformational leadership because he values the relationship-building aspects it promotes. In addition, he has been a mental health and substance abuse counselor for more than three years at various facilities and under several managers. One of the managers was transactional, and one was transformational. Another manager employed both transactional and transformational leadership styles. The researcher bracketed these biases and experiences. Be aware of biases, try to set them aside, and be open to all possible data that is collected.

During this process, the author served as the main individual transcribing, coding, and reviewing emergent themes. This method ensures that the author is fully immersed and knowledgeable of the data (Castelberry & Nolen, 2018). After the data was explored, reviewed, and coded, the author reviewed the data using a framework matrix tool in NVivo. This allowed the author to review themes expressed by the participants and explore, in a condensed format, how these themes relate to the research questions of this study (Castelberry & Nolen, 2018). NVivo also provided a tool to illustrate themes using word charts and cluster analyses. These tools were used if they benefited the exploration and presentation of the data within this dissertation. After coding the research, the author analyzed and interpreted the codes and themes that emerged from thematic analysis per Braun and Clarke (2006). Resultant themes from thematic analysis were used to address the research questions proposed in this dissertation. This included establishing clear lines of evidence by demonstrating exemplifying textual data that provides answers regarding the research questions. Finally, these themes were used to draw conclusions regarding the research questions by using the thematic analysis conducted for this study (Bengtsson, 2016). There were no triangulation efforts due to a lack of time and financial resources for this project.

Assumptions

The main assumption within this study is that participants were able to provide information regarding the leadership of mental health care counselors and managers. This assumption was based on the knowledge these groups have direct interaction with each other and that health care managers lead their subordinate counselors. These participants may be unable to provide information regarding leadership. In this case, more participants would be recruited for this study. The other possible assumption was that participants would respond to questions in an honest manner. It was not possible to detect if participants were not truthful. However, the participants were made to feel comfortable, assured of their confidentially, and all interviews were conducted outside their workplaces. Conducting interviews in a place other than their work ensured the participants of confidentiality and provided comfort during the interview.

Limitations

The first limitation of this study was that it focused on only two mental health care facilities. Assessing the participants from these facilities only garnered information related to these specific facilities. However, through thematic analysis, the resulting themes would be ideally indicated as general ideas concerning transformational and transactional leadership styles. This could lead to a more comprehensive understanding of how they are utilized by some mental health care counselors and managers.

The second limitation was that study participants were limited to those who chose to volunteer for this study. This ensured that participants were voluntarily providing information and felt comfortable in the study. However, this also meant it was not possible to review the total number of participants until all voluntary participants responded to the email request. This limitation was acceptable as this methodology ensured that all participants were voluntary, and they were assured of their safety.

Delimitations

There were two delimitations noted in this study. First, participants who participated in this study had to have a minimum of five years of experience and a CASC's counseling certification or a license in social work. These criteria ensured that participants were qualified and had experience working in the field having been managed or as a manager. Individuals who were new to the field might not be able to provide sufficient information regarding the research questions.

The delimitation of the population was mental health care counselors and mental health managers. Multiple practices within the mental health care field can be addressed (e.g., psychologists). However, leadership involving mental health care counselors and mental health managers has yet to be addressed in scholarly literature. Thus this delimitation is acceptable as it fills a gap in the current body of scholarly literature.

Ethical Assurances

Ethical assurances were maintained for this study in multiple ways. First, the study requested approval from the IRB. The study did not proceed until IRB approval was granted. The researcher gained approval to conduct interviews with the HR official of the chosen mental health care facility, and then IRB approval was obtained for the purpose of the study. When HR approval was received, emails were sent by someone other than the administrator to assure no coercion. For example, the secretary forwarded my email requesting participation to the mental health counselors and managers within the facilities. The participants were informed their responses and identities would be confidential; pseudonyms were provided for all materials. The participants were also informed of IRB and HR approval. Participants were also informed that the study was voluntary, and they could exit the interviews at any point.

During the interviews, participants were again reminded that their responses were confidential, and they could voluntarily leave at any point. I also provided participants with a written copy of the confidentiality information before the interviews, which they had to sign.

All data for this project, including digital USB data and handwritten and recorded notes were kept in a locked file cabinet in the researcher's office. The researcher was the only person with access to this cabinet. Digital data stored on the researcher's computer was password-protected. Data analysis did not occur in a public place or anywhere that could compromise participant confidentiality. All data analysis occurred in a private place, such as in the researcher's home office. Per IRB requirements, project data will be destroyed after five years. This will include the deletion of all digital files and the destruction of the USB device used for this study.

The final ethical consideration is the personal bias of the researcher. This bias was mitigated by keeping a personal journal during the entire process of data collection regarding instances of possible bias. This form of bracketing is designed to ensure that researcher bias can be mitigated to the fullest extent possible (Peters & Halcomb, 2015; Sorsa, Kikkala, & Astedt-Kurki, 2015). The researcher did not have personal experience with this topic. But the bracketing system allowed the researcher to monitor for bias during data collection and analysis.

Summary

This chapter presented the research methodology for this study. An introduction to the study and brief review of the proposed topic were discussed. The purpose of the study was also reviewed in this section. The following section, research methodology and design, discussed the use of a qualitative descriptive methodology. This section also noted that a thematic analysis design was utilized. The section provided detailed information regarding the method for thematic analysis and IRB permission for this study. The use of a qualitative methodology was justified in accordance with the research questions.

The population and sample were reviewed and relevant demographic information for the sample discussed. The sample and sample saturation were also justified in this section in accordance with the research questions. Following was a discussion of the data collection instrument for this study, which is the author. The interview questions were discussed as well.

Study procedures were subsequently assessed and reviewed. This section assessed the methodology for collecting data and from who the data was collected. The following section, "Data Collection and Analysis," discussed the exact strategies used to code, analyze, transcribe, and interpret the resultant data. The last sections of this study reviewed the assumptions, delimitations, and ethical assurance of this study. The assumptions were reviewed to assess the assumed variables for the study. The delimitations section reviewed the purposeful delimitations imposed on the study to gather data specific to the research questions.

Limitations of the study were then reviewed. This included the limitations that could exist regarding the data collection and analysis for this study.

CHAPTER 4

Results

This study strives to fill gaps in research and literature related to the relationships between counselors and managers in the mental health field by investigating if, how, and to what effect transformational and transactional leadership styles are used in the mental health field, thereby potentially impacting the effectiveness of the individuals. The researcher employed qualitative analysis strategies to gain insight into the perspectives of both counselors and managers working in mental health facilities. Semi-structured interviews were conducted among five counselors and four managers, seeking answers to the following research questions:

RQ1. From the perspective of counselors and managers, what transformational managerial tactics produce positive work outcomes?

RQ2. From the perspective of counselors and managers, what transformational managerial tactics produce positive relationships between the counselor and the manager?

RQ3. From the perspective of counselors and managers, what transactional managerial tactics producing positive work outcomes?

RQ4. From the perspective of counselors and managers, what transactional managerial tactics produce positive relationships between the counselor and the manager?

Qualitative thematic analysis was utilized to extract meaning from the interview responses. Recurring themes identified by the researcher through the analysis process will be presented in this chapter as the findings of the study.

This chapter begins with a discussion of study demographics followed by a description of the data collection strategies employed. Data analysis methods are also discussed, along with the efforts taken to ensure study trustworthiness, before turning to the presentation of findings. Findings include detailed descriptions of researcher-identified themes supported by direct quotations from interview responses.

Demographics

The population of this study consisted of counselors and managers currently employed at either the New York Hope Center or the New York Substance Abuse Facility. These facilities were selected due to the researcher's accessibility to counselors in those locations. To qualify for participation in the study, individuals needed to meet the following requirements: actively employed at one of the two health facilities previously designated, five or more years of experience in the mental health services field, and either CASC's counseling certification or a comparable license in social work. Nine participants completed interviews for this study, including five counselors and four managers. No additional demographic information was collected.

Data Collection

Approval from the researcher's IRB, as well as the administration of the facilities from which participants were recruited, were obtained prior to initiating data collection. Participants were identified and invited to participate in this study via email. On receipt of administrative approval to utilize their organizations to recruit participants, the researcher provided the HR departments of each facility with a copy of the invitation email. This introductory email served to inform potential participants of the purpose of the study, as well as the roles of the researcher and the participants. The email also included copies of the IRB and HR approval letters, along with informed consent documentation. Potential participants were assured that measures would be taken to ensure participant protection and confidentiality, and participation would remain entirely voluntary throughout the study. Participants were also notified that each would receive a $10 Amazon gift card for their participation in the study. Participants who were interested in joining the study were encouraged to contact the researcher via email. Subsequently, the researcher scheduled interviews with all willing participants. All participants submitted an informed consent form prior to initiating their participation in the study.

The researcher constructed a semi-structured interview guide to assist in the data collection process (appendix C). Prior to beginning data collection, the interview guide was field-tested via a phone interview with a mental health counselor. Responses to the pilot interview were used to verify the credibility and effectiveness of the questions; responses to the pilot interview were not included in the data population of this study. Interviews were conducted at a time convenient to the participant. All interviews were conducted via phone, utilizing the GoogleVoice application to record the interview. The researcher also took handwritten notes to supplement the recordings.

On completion, each interview was transcribed into text using the online transcription service REV. Transcripts were then returned to the participants for checking, allowing each participant an opportunity to verify that the transcript was an accurate and authentic representation of his or her experiences and opinions. The researcher maintained participant confidentiality by assigning pseudonyms to each participant according to their roles in the mental health field. Counselors were assigned a pseudonym consisting of the letter C and a numerical value (C1, C2, C3, C4, or C5). Manager pseudonyms were composed of the letter M and a numerical value (M1, M2, M3, and M4).

Data Analysis

At the completion of the data collection process, the researcher utilized thematic analysis to organize and extract meaning from within the data. To begin the analysis process, the researcher uploaded each interview text into NVivo, the data analysis software used to facilitate data organization and the analysis process. The researcher then conducted a preliminary reading of each text in full. During this process, the researcher was able to familiarize himself with the data and begin to take note of any recurring subjects or themes. Once the researcher had familiarized himself with the data, he began the coding process.

Coding was the process used to organize the data according to inductively identified themes and patterns within the texts. NVivo software facilitated the process by enabling the researcher to code key words and phrases that were then able to be viewed and manipulated in subsequent rounds of coding. Following the initial round of coding, the researcher continued to review each text, assigning and refining code groups where necessary. With each subsequent round of coding, the researcher further refined each coding group until the groups that remained were reflective of the primary recurring subjects and shared experiences of the responses.

On the completion of assigning codes, the researcher reviewed the coding groups one last time, comparing the groups to the data population as a whole to ensure that the groups remained an authentic representation of the data. The coding groups that remained represent the common themes and shared experiences identified within the responses. In the subsequent sections of this chapter, these themes will be discussed organized according to the form of leadership strategies to which they relate.

Trustworthiness

To ensure the research and findings remained trustworthy, the researcher took various measures to establish credibility of the study. The researcher conducted the data collection and analysis personally to remain fully immersed in the data and ensure familiarity with the responses on which this study's findings are based. By completing member checking of the interview texts, the researcher strove to ensure that the interview texts remained authentic and accurate representations of the participant perceptions and experiences, and uninfluenced by potential misrepresentation or bias from the researcher. The dependability of the findings was supported by conducting a pilot interview prior to initiating data collection, thereby enabling the researcher to test his interview guides and ensure that the interview questions would yield responses applicable to the study's research questions.

Because all participants were employees of either the New York Hope Center or the New York Substance Abuse Facility, the study's findings may not be considered directly transferrable to alternative populations. To overcome this limitation, the researcher described his research design, data collection, and analysis processes in detail so that future studies among alternative populations may replicate this study's methods, thereby expanding the school of literature related to transactional and transformational leadership styles within the mental health field. As the present study aimed to expand the understanding of transformational and transactional leadership within the mental health field, the researcher hopes that the study will be replicated with different populations and settings in order to gain additional insight into the applicability of such leadership styles in the broader mental health field.

Results

In the following sections, themes that were identified through qualitative thematic analysis are discussed. Each theme is depicted with detailed descriptions. Quotations from interview responses are provided to help substantiate each theme. The following discussion is organized according to the two leadership styles discussed: transformational and transactional.

Themes Related to Transformational Leadership Strategies

Response analysis revealed that participants feel that transformational leadership tactics help to boost employee morale and create a positive work environment. Five of the nine participants expressed beliefs that transformational leadership tactics help to improve the morale of mental health workers and, therefore, their team. Participants highlighted the motivational aspects related to transformational leadership, which contributed to a positive work environment for both employees and clients. For example, in discussing their experiences with transformational leadership in their workplaces, C1 described the experience as, "It works. [Transformational leadership] boosts morale." Similarly, C4 described experiences with transformational leadership: "I could tell you it just makes me a happy person. It makes me want to come to work. I come here every day happy. I come here feeling supported." Both examples depict the perspective of counselors that transformational leadership contributes to a positive work experience and team environment.

Managers also highlighted the ability of transformational leadership tactics to contribute to a positive work environment. Some managers described the construction of a comfortable work environment for their employees in which leadership helps counselors to be motivated and made to feel comfortable in their roles. For example, M3 described utilizing transformational leadership strategies in terms of creating a positive work environment, stating: "If the environment is healthy and the environment is comfortable, everyone is willing to do the work. This should not be a job that you don't want to come to work and do. This should be a job that you really enjoy doing because you are servicing the community."

M3's statement explains the personal belief that by using transformational leadership to establish a positive work environment, managers can increase worker satisfaction and productivity. Similarly, M4 described one particular example of transformational leadership experiences resulting in an increase in an employee's confidence in her role. The manager explained: "She's been able to sit in her own groups after a while, and then I'm able to look back at the notes and see where she applied what we spoke about and how she applied it. And she did very well. I was able to compliment her on it. And I think that helped her, boosted her, made her feel more comfortable. Because the more comfortable you feel in your work, the better you do at it."

M4's example describes the connection between utilizing transformational leadership to support employees and the increase in confidence and comfort that may result in increased employee effectiveness.

Participants feel that transformational leadership tactics help counselors to feel supported and encouraged by supervisors. Seven participants, including three counselors and four managers, expressed that they feel transformational leadership tactics help employees to feel supported and encouraged by managers. For example, C4 described the manager's use of transformational leadership tactics as, "He's extremely supportive in everything that we do. And even when we do something wrong, he'll say, 'Well, you know what? You could use that. But how about this way? Think about working this way. Think about how the client would feel this way.'"

C4 described the ways in which the manager is able to support his employees by providing encouragement and support, even when they do something wrong. C4 continued, "And just because he gave me that support, I'm telling you, I came back, and I think I did a better job because I felt so supported and so loved." C4 clearly describes the perception that the amount of support received from the manager was directly related to success in the job.

C3 described a similar experience, stating that the manager is, "willing to work with me while I'm learning, while I'm going through a learning process. [My manager] is very motivational." This statement expresses the belief that the manager uses transformational leadership tactics to motivate and encourage employees, providing support throughout the learning process.

Managers also highlighted the role of providing employees with support and encouragement in utilizing transformational leadership tactics. For example, M1 described the understanding and use of transformational leadership this way:

> So if I was to look at transformational leadership, approaches are to find out what individuals like, encourage what they like, and guide them to where I need them to be for the company. Then we meet somewhere in the middle, where they're feeling supported, and the company is getting what it needs in terms of exchange for their compensation ... the ability to see that their hard work is not going unnoticed through encouraging emails, through encouraging talks that I'd have with them, through supervision.

This explanation demonstrates the growth-related aspects of transformational leadership. M1 emphasized the importance of identifying employee interests and skills and providing support and encouragement in order for employees to grow in a direction that will benefit both staff and organization.

M3 described another example of using transformational tactics to support employees through tasks they may be less comfortable with: "I make the environment comfortable so that employees can feel comfortable to ask me any questions about anything they don't have any knowledge of. I give them my experience, and I'll sit with them and help them go through because I believe some of the best experience is learned through practicing this craft that we have."

M3's explanation emphasizes the importance of supporting employees by providing hands-on assistance and support when necessary to help them grow in skills and confidence.

Participants felt that clear communication contributes to positive transformational leadership experiences. Seven of the nine participants also expressed a belief that clear communication between counselors and their managers is important in transformational leadership experiences. For example, regarding transformational leadership tactics that they've experienced, C1 stated, "You have somebody that's constantly telling you, 'Look, you're doing a good job,' letting you know if you're not doing a good job, or what areas that you could do better." This statement depicts an environment in which the manager regularly communicates with the employee, providing feedback to encourage and enhance the success of their staff.

C4 described a similar experience related to receiving communication and feedback from their manager: "[My manager] tells you the truth about everything. So if you're slacking somewhere, he's going to tell you. But he always tells you in such a way, 'Listen, this is how this is going to affect you. So what do you want?'"

Additionally, C5 stated, "The positive relationship outcome [of transformational leadership] was we had a much clearer communication path when it came to work." Each of these responses demonstrate a counselor perception that transformational leadership and clear communication are related and can contribute to positive work outcomes.

Each of the four managers who participated in the study also expressed a relationship between clear communication with their employees and positive transformational leadership experiences. For example, M4 stated, "I believe in being open with them, letting them know that I've been through what you've been through, and this is how I was able to work through it. This may work more for you. It may not, but I would give it a try." Such a statement, referring to the manager's ability to be open with his or her employees when it comes to offering management or guidance, demonstrates his or her belief that transformational leadership requires an avenue for openly and clearly communicating with employees.

M3 described a similar belief:

> I'm a firm believer that people learn more from watching somebody do something than someone telling them what to do. If I'm leading, I'm being positive, healthy. If they can see that I have some flaws, too, and that I make mistakes, they'll feel comfortable thinking, *Well, he made mistakes, too, and he recognizes his mistakes.* And when I confront a counselor about something that I may have been misinformed

about what they did, if I'm wrong, I come back to say, "You know what, I humbly apologize. I misunderstood. All is forgiven." So it's a healthy environment here.

As M3 explained, transformational leadership strategies rely on the manager's ability to communicate and relate to his or her employees by providing hands-on guidance and firsthand advice. Not only do managers need to communicate with their employees about the actions, responsibilities, and tasks, communication should be a two-way-street in which managers are willing to admit their mistakes or shortcomings too.

Another example of a manager's perceptions of transformational leadership and communication with employees can be found in M1's explanation of individual beliefs and strategies:

> So there were staff when I started who were timid about voicing their concerns. I created an environment that it was okay to confront me as long as it was done in a respectful manner, but really giving them the ability to just have that voice, the ability to trust, the ability to see that their hard work is not going unnoticed through encouraging emails, through encouraging talks that I'd have with them through supervision.

M1 emphasizes the importance of establishing a comfortable environment and relationship with the employees so that communication can flow freely. M1's comments suggest that employees will be more effective and more content with work if they have the ability to communicate openly with their supervisors.

Participants feel transformational leadership tactics contribute to increased productivity and employee effectiveness. All four managers expressed a belief that transformational leadership strategies have resulted in an increase in employee productivity or effectiveness. For example, regarding outcomes related to the use of transformational leadership strategies, M1 stated, "I can say that productivity has increased at least by 30 percent since I've been here, and that's through no additional expenses to the company. That's just through excitement and drive and people just understanding what the goal is, knowing that there is a process here that might be somewhat positive. There's a partnership that occurs where it's symbiotic."

M1's statement describes the ways in which transformational leadership can bring about positive outcomes in the workplace by increasing worker satisfaction and productivity while not increasing organization expenses. Similarly, M2 described their experience from when they first arrived in the manager role to now:

> Staff was feeling unappreciated, unmotivated, and it was a revolving door. I've been in this field since 2009, so I've watched this revolving door effect from [transactional] types of leadership. Luckily I had a good supervisor that grew me into [transformational] leadership style. So I took that with my own style and then brought that to the field to actually motivate and inspire.

M2 provides an interesting look into his or her organization's experience and success with different types of leadership styles. As M2's explain, employees felt underappreciated and unmotivated when transformational leadership was lacking.

When the participant entered the management role, he or she was able to improve the situation by using transformational leadership strategies to motivate and inspire staff.

M3 describes the positive outcomes he or she has experienced through transformational experience by highlighting an increase in employee comfort levels, resulting in higher employee confidence levels and better care:

> By making the environment comfortable for them to be able to ask all the questions, they're starting to feel more confident. They're okay with making mistakes because they're understanding that mistakes are the best way to learn how to do things correctly. And when they do make a mistake and I confront them with it, they know that I'm not confronting them, the person. I'm confronting what they did so that they can remember not to do it again. They understand that it's practice, and they practice the craft. They stay a little later; sometimes they come a little early. And their notes and their documentation have improved. And when they're feeling good about themselves, their clients feel that their counselor is confident.

As M3 explained, when employees are confident about their skills and abilities to serve their clients, this results in better care and more satisfied clients as well, which is made possible due to transformational leadership.

Participants feel that transformational leadership tactics contribute to higher rates of staff retention. Two of the four managers highlighted an improvement in staff retention numbers as a result of using transformational leadership strategies. Regarding positive outcomes resulting from transformational leadership, M1 stated, "Staff retention has been tremendous, and since the three years that I've been here, if two people exited because they, 'found something greener,' on the other side, that'd be a lot. The team that works in this facility right now has been here for a very long time."

M1's statement demonstrates that staff satisfaction has increased as a result of transformational leadership strategies, leading to relatively little turnover due to burnout. Similarly, M2 described the positive outcomes related to transformational leadership in comparison with transactional leadership strategies: "Staff was feeling unappreciated, unmotivated, and it was a revolving door. Staff turnover rates, things like that. If I had to put it in a percentage of staff turnover rate, in [transactional] management, used to be at like 60 to 70 percent. That's high."

M2 refers to the low retention rates amid transactional leadership efforts as a, "revolving door." However, he or she also describes how he or she was able to utilize transformational leadership to motivate and inspire his or her employees.

Themes Related to Transactional Leadership Tactics

Participants felt that transactional leadership contributes to employee independence or confidence. Three participants expressed the belief that transactional leaderships strategies can contribute to increased employee independence. When describing the leadership strategies they prefer to receive from their managers, C3 described transactional leadership as their preferred type of leadership due to the ability to avoid being micromanaged: "It goes back to how I'm told the assignment. If someone's on top of me, I don't react very. If someone gives me a task and says, 'Okay, give this a try. Try and do it yourself, and if you have questions come to me,' I'm good with that because I feel more that I'm doing it myself, and I'm not being led on like I'm five."

C3's statement depicts his or her preference to have a more hands-off management approach, which transactional tends to provide as compared to transformational leadership experiences. Similarly, C5 described the ways in which transactional leadership impacted his or her role in the mental health field, stating, "Transactional leadership can actually be beneficial in one way, like it forced me to make decisions and just, based on my own experience, decisions that I felt were going to be best for the client. So it actually boosted my own confidence in the decisions that I was making."

C5's statement demonstrates the positive outcome of transactional leadership, resulting in a necessity to make decisions and act independently from a manager, ultimately leading to an increase in confidence in his or her personal skills and decision-making.

Participants felt that offering rewards or punishments to employees promotes positive outcomes. Managers described the various systems of rewards and punishments they have used as a part of transactional leadership strategies to promote positive outcomes. Incentives under transactional leadership strategies included vacation policy, overtime policy, credentials, and compensation. For example, M1 described his or her transaction leadership strategies as, "The whole aspect of the money, allowing them time off, that if they want to take a vacation, one of the things I tell them is that they need to plan their paperwork. That's essentially transactional. Their vacation is kind of up in the air until they are able to show significantly that this treatment plan will be taken care of by this counselor, to make sure that the paperwork and compliance is still 100 percent."

He or she also described his or her overtime policy as a transactional motivation, stating, "I would tell the staff, 'Listen, if you make sixty services a week, and you want to stay an extra hour or two, as long as you hit that sixty, I'll approve your overtime, but you have to be providing a service.'"

Despite highlighting these strategies as forms of transactional leadership that have resulted in positive outcomes, M1 also highlighted the limits of transactional leadership strategies such as these:

> These strategies are definitely transactional. And they've worked, but it's kind of a one and done. It's one of those things that once the money goes away, the extra services will go away. Where transformational, I think is a lot stronger than that. That there doesn't need to be that money. There'd have to be a lot of succession of things to happen in order for transformational leadership to fade away as opposed to transactional leadership, or outcomes from transactional leadership to fade away.

In this way, M1 highlights his or her opinion of the effectiveness of transactional and transformational leadership strategies. While the use of rewards and punishment may bring about results in employees, those results are more likely to be short-lived and rely on the provision of a reward when compared to transformational leadership strategies.

M3 described his or her experience with encouraging employee effectiveness through the encouragement of obtaining credentials: "What we're trying to do here is promote counselors who are credentialed, so we want to provide them with the necessary training. The skill set to increase through the work—documentation, computers, and counseling skills—because the more credentialed the counselors, the more experienced the counselors are, the better it helps the agency."

M3's statement described the way his or her organization utilizes obtaining higher credentials as a transactional leadership incentive, promising promotion, an increase in skill set, or even an increase in compensation related to putting in the time and effort to obtain additional credentials.

Participants felt that transactional leadership contributes to increased employee effectiveness. In addition to feeling that the use of transactional leadership rewards may contribute to positive work outcomes, managers also expressed a belief that it may contribute to increased employee effectiveness. For example, M3 described an experience with an employee who was trained to improve her note-taking ability through transactional leadership strategies:

> I used to let [the counselor] type the note, with me dictating. As a result of her listening to me dictate what she needs to put in these progress notes—the content, the assessment, and the plan—she has so much experience in documenting these notes that, to be quite honest, her documentation is a little better than mine now. So she has a reward. The reward is experience, and she is very good at documentation, the wording and everything.

Despite the fact that this meant additional work for the counselor, the reward of having increased experience was offered. As a result, the counselor was able to expand her skill set through the use of the manager's transactional leadership strategy.

M4 described a similar experience with his or her counselor. He or she explained that by asking his or her counselor to manage client groups on his or her own, the counselor was rewarded with an increase in confidence and skills related to his or her role in the organization. The manager summed up this example by stating, "The confidence that was built, it shows in the work, allowing her to do what she does on her own, and then giving positive feedback when she does something well has led to positive work outcomes." M4 stated that the positive outcome is evident in the improved work of the employee due to the manager's willingness to provide the counselor with personal experience without hands-on assistance from the manager.

M1 also described a positive outcome from transactional leadership that is related to increased employee effectiveness. He or she stated that transactional leadership has led to an increase in worker productivity, which is evident through "bigger numbers" when it comes time to reporting: "I've had staff that went from seventy services a week to one hundred. I've had staff that went from 100 to 130. How does that impact them? They get more money. They're able to maybe purchase better things that they want or pay off bills that maybe were hanging over their heads. So in that aspect, the benefits are they get a bigger paycheck. From my standpoint, I get bigger numbers to report to my bosses." Due to the use of transactional leadership efforts, including the incentive of a larger paycheck for employees, the organization has been able to greatly increase their productivity per employee, as demonstrated by the numbers listed above.

Counselors felt that transactional leadership tactics were less effective. Six of the nine participants expressed discontent with transactional leadership strategies or a preference for transformational leadership in their responses. For example, C2 stated that he or she disagreed with the idea of transactional leadership because employees should be intrinsically motivated and should not require an incentive in the form of a reward or punishment. C2 stated, "I think as a counselor, whatever you do, you should be just doing it to reward yourself at the end of the day because this is what you love to do. It shouldn't be really about getting anything. This is your career. It should always be rewarding just seeing your patients making change or you made a difference or you helped. That's what should be the reward at the end of the day."

C1 also expressed the sentiment that employees should not depend on rewards to determine their work ethic: "[Transactional leadership] is not a great leadership to me. Tit-for-tat. There should be no tit for tat. You do this, I do that. No, you have a job to do, and at the end of the day, you get paid to do a job. So at the end of the day, that's what it is. You give me a task; my task is to do what you asked me to do. It shouldn't be that you have to offer me a reward."

Other counselors expressed negative experiences with transactional leadership, leading them to perceive transactional leadership as less effective than other forms of leadership. For example, C3 described his or her experiences with transactional leadership and his or her perception that it did not yield positive results: "I find my immediate supervisor is transactional. [They tell us] 'All right, well, if you're behind on this, we'll send you to the Bronx one day, where you won't see everybody, and we'll put you on lockdown until things get done.' Stuff like that. It's the way it's presented to me. I feel undermined."

According to C3's statement, his or her manager's use of transactional leadership is focused more on punishment rather than reward. Rather than feeling supported or encouraged by the manager, C3 considered the transactional leadership experience negatively.

C4 described his or her experience with transactional leadership as, "When you just leave me with a job, and you just walk away, I don't know if I did the job right. I don't know what I've accomplished. I have no idea." This statement suggests that transactional leadership, where managers tend to be more hands-off, can lead to employee discontent or lack of confidence.

Two managers also expressed the sentiment that transactional leadership styles are not effective. M3 described his or her experience with transactional leadership, in which insufficient guidance or support was provided, resulting in long-term negative impacts on the employees and the service to clients:

> I don't think we should ever leave our supervisee with the task without explaining it to them early in this field. They used to throw us to the wolves, and we'd just have to figure it out on our own. And based on my experience with that, a lot of counselors developed some bad habits that led to them to do certain things the wrong way for so many years that when new regulations come up, they don't want to conform to the new regulations. They don't want to change.

Similarly, M 2 described transactional leadership as a detriment to the mental health field:

> I don't really see a positive from [transactional leadership]. That's the detriment. It's more of a detriment to the actual field and the actual counselors. If I'm the manager and I'm transactional, the counselor is going to be transactional toward the client. And that's not the best approach because clients are already feeling like they're cut out of society, they're not welcomed, nobody really cares. So bringing that type of approach just solidifies that behavior.

M2's statement suggests that transactional leadership serves to reinforce negative behavior rather than promote positive outcomes by encouraging counselors to use transactional tactics with their clients. M3 continued, "I've been in the field long enough to see the detriments with the transactional approach, and it's not something that works in this field."

Summary

In this chapter, the results of the qualitative research on mental health workers' experiences and perceptions of transactional and transformational leadership styles was presented. First, demographic data pertinent to the study was presented. Next, the data collection and analysis strategies employed in this study were described in detail. Semi-structured interviews conducted among five mental health counselors and four mental health managers were used to collect the data for this study. All participants were actively employed by either New York Hope Center or New York Substance Abuse Facility and possessed five or more years' experience in the mental health field. Participants were recruited via email, with permission and assistance from the facilities' human resources departments. Nine interviews were conducted, and the responses of these interviews formed the data population of the study.

On completion of the data collection, qualitative thematic analysis was conducted on the data. NVivo software was used to assist in the data organization and analysis process. The researcher reviewed the data repeatedly, conducting multiple rounds of coding to extract meaning and identify themes within the responses. The themes that resulted from analysis make up the findings presented in this chapter, organized according to this study's research questions:

RQ1. From the perspective of counselors and managers, what transformational managerial tactics produce positive work outcomes?

RQ2. From the perspective of counselors and managers, what transformational managerial tactics produce positive relationships between the counselor and the manager?

RQ3. From the perspective of counselors and managers, what transactional managerial tactics produce positive work outcomes?

RQ4. From the perspective of counselors and managers, what transactional managerial tactics produce positive relationships between the counselor and the manager?

Themes were presented with detailed descriptions and quotations from the interview responses to support each finding. The study found that mental health workers found transformational leadership strategies more effective than transactional leadership strategies. Transformational leadership strategies were perceived by participants to help foster a positive work environment and provide support and encouragement to employees. Clear communication was perceived to be related to successful transformational leadership experiences. Transformational leadership strategies were perceived to increase worker productivity and effectiveness, as well as increase worker retention rates within the organization.

On the other hand, themes related to transactional leadership strategies included participant perceptions that transactional leadership can bring increased independence and confidence within mental health counselors. Additionally, although transactional leadership does have the potential to increase worker productivity, many participants expressed beliefs that it is less effective at producing positive outcomes or relationships. These results will be considered further in the next chapter as the implications of these findings are discussed and recommendations for the mental health field and future studies are provided.

CHAPTER 5

Implications, Recommendations, and Conclusions

The purpose of this qualitative research was to explore how transactional and transformational leadership influence the counselor and manager relationship in mental health counseling settings. This study was conducted to address the problem that, although there is a significant body of research on leadership in business contexts (Smith & Khojasteh, 2014), there is a gap in the literature regarding the leadership relationship between counselors and managers in the mental health field (Bowen & Moore, 2014). As a result of that gap in literature, mental health counselors and managers lacked evidence-based, field-specific guidance for developing leader-follower relationships (Hesler, 2018). To address the gap in the literature and contribute insights and recommendations for practitioners and future researchers, this study was undertaken to explore the leadership styles used in the mental health field and the effects of those styles.

The conceptual framework in this study was drawn from the literature on the transformational and transactional leadership styles. Transformational leadership was defined as a leadership style that enhances followers' motivations, satisfaction, and performances by inspiring them to work toward a collective vision (Breevaart & Bakker, 2018). Components of transformational leadership include idealized influence, in which the leader models desired behaviors and attitudes in order to lead by example; inspirational motivation, in which leaders employ charisma and clear communication to win follower buy-in to a values-congruent vision that transcends individual interests; individualized consideration, in which leaders place a high priority on followers' personal needs and self-actualization, and; intellectual stimulation, in which leaders motivate followers to exceed expectations and realize their full potential (Breevaart & Bakker, 2018; Muchiri et al., 2019; Nazim, 2016). Transactional leadership contrasts with the focus on transformational leadership on inspirational motivation, in that it involves harnessing followers' self-interests to promote collective goals through quid pro quo incentives based on individual rewards (Nazim, 2016).

The specific gap in the literature to be addressed in the present study was the lack of previous research on whether and to what degree mental health managers use transformational and transactional leadership styles in their relationships with counselors, and how those leadership styles influence counselor-manager relationships in a mental health setting (see Bowen & Moore, 2014).

To address the research problem, a qualitative methodology and descriptive design were selected. Data was collected through semi-structured interviews with nine managers and counselors employed at two centers for addiction and mental health care. The two centers were given pseudonyms to preserve site anonymity and referred to in this study as the New York Hope Center and the New York Substance Abuse Facility. Audio-recorded interview data were transcribed verbatim, uploaded into NVivo software, and analyzed using a thematic procedure.

The major themes that emerged to answer the four research questions are discussed in detail in the "Implications" section of this chapter. As a preliminary overview, the findings indicated that mental health care workers perceived the transformational leadership style as more effective than the transactional style. Participants perceived the inspirational motivation component of transformational leadership as effective in increasing counselor productivity, morale, and retention. Participants perceived individualized consideration as conducive to positive counselor-manager relationships. Transactional leadership was perceived as effective for promoting short-term productivity, as well as for promoting skill and credential acquisition that would have long-term benefits. However, transactional leadership was perceived as potentially detrimental to long-term counselor-manager and counselor-client relationships.

The following section discusses the implications of the findings in this study in relation to the research questions, study problem, study purpose. Their relationships to previous literature are addressed. The chapter then includes recommendations for practice. This section is a description and discussion of how the findings in this study can be used as a guide to improve leadership practices in mental health care settings. Recommendations for future research based on the limitations and findings in this study are provided. The final section of this chapter is a statement of conclusions.

Implications

This section discusses how the findings in this study address the research questions, research problem, and relate to previous relevant literature. It is organized by research question. Within the discussion related to each research question, major themes from the findings are discussed.

RQ1: From the perspectives of counselors and managers, what transformational managerial tactics produce positive work outcomes? The findings used to answer this research question addressed the research problem and the study purpose by extending the otherwise well-tested findings of previous researchers to a mental health care context in which they had not previously been confirmed. Three major themes emerged during data analysis to answer this research question. The first relevant theme was: Participants feel that transformational leadership tactics help to boost employee morale and create a positive work environment. Participants expressed the perception that the inspirational motivation component of transformational leadership has the effect of improving the morale of mental health care workers and creates a more positive work environment for workers and clients. This finding was consistent with those of researchers such as Breevaart and Bakker (2018) and Muchiri et al. (2019), who described the inspirational motivation component of transformational leadership as increasing employee morale significantly by producing job commitment and alignment of individuals with collective goals.

The second relevant theme was: Participants feel that transformational leadership tactics contribute to increased productivity and effectiveness of employees. This theme indicated that the inspirational motivation practices of clearly communicating goals and gaining buy-in from followers enhanced employee job performance. This finding was consistent with those of previous researchers, who have emphasized the importance of clear communication as a component of effective leadership (e.g., Afsar et al., 2017; Antonakis & Day, 2017), as well as with the findings of researchers who have indicated that inspirational motivation is unlikely to occur if the leader does not clearly, consistently, and charismatically convey a vision (Breevaart & Bakker, 2018; Muchiri et al., 2019; Nazim, 2016). These findings added to the previous literature that inspirational motivation involving clear communication in a mental health care setting had a significance that participants described indicated some previous managers overlooked. To effectively enhance employee motivation, it was necessary for managers to communicate clear, specific, collective goals rather than to assume the goals of counseling were sufficiently implied by the function of the profession.

The third relevant theme was: Participants feel that transformational leadership tactics contribute to higher rates of staff retention. The finding that inspirational motivation reduces employee burnout and turnover by increasing employee morale has been consistently confirmed in the literature on transformational leadership (e.g., Bhugra et al., 2013; Corrigan et al., 2002; Gable, 2012; Heok, 2010; Singh, 2000). Theme 3 added to the previous literature represented through the high importance participants placed on counselors' subjective experiences of their workplaces. For example, in stating of inspirational motivation, "It just makes me a happy person. It makes me want to come to work. I come here every day happy," C4 expressed an experience that contrasted with characterizations in the literature of mental health care workplaces as conducive to an elevated incidence of burnout and turnover (e.g., Holman et al., 2018; Quintana & Cabrera, 2015; Schilling et al., 2018). The importance counselors and managers placed on employees' job satisfaction and on the creation of a positive work environment was consistent with the findings of previous researchers, but it extended those findings by suggesting that transformational leadership involving inspirational motivation may be an effective means of preventing or alleviating burnout and attrition among mental health care workers.

RQ2. From the perspective of counselors and managers, what transformational managerial tactics produce positive relationships between the counselor and the manager? Two major themes emerged during data analysis to answer this question. The first relevant theme was that participants felt transformational leadership tactics help counselors to feel supported and encouraged by supervisors. Data associated with this theme indicated that managers' individualized consideration in supporting and encouraging counselors contributed to positive counselor-manager relationships and, by doing so, improved counselors' job performance. This finding was consistent with those of researchers such as Breevaart and Bakker (2018), who indicated that individualized consideration facilitates follower motivation and identification with a collective vision by validating and addressing their personal needs for support and self-actualization. The finding is also consistent with those of Gable (2012), who concluded that managerial support and encouragement of mental health care workers is an effective means of meeting the specific needs of counselors.

In data associated with theme 1, participants focused on the personal and relational significance of direct supervisory support and encouragement. In saying of the effects of a manager's direct support and encouragement, "I felt so supported and so loved" (C4), and, "[counselors are] feeling supported" (M1), participants emphasized the subjective aspect of counselors' experiences of individualized consideration. As with findings in this study that mental health care managers' transformational leadership increased counselor morale, productivity, and retention, the finding that transformational leadership helps counselors to feel their managers' support and encourage them indicated that the direct and most significant effect of transformational practices was to improve counselors' subjective experiences of the workplace. Leadership practices that made counselors happier, participants believed, exerted a decisive influence on morale, performance, the quality of counselor-manager relationships, and retention versus turnover.

The second theme relevant to RQ2 was: Participants feel that clear communication contributes to positive transformational leadership experiences. Data associated with this theme indicated that managers' individualized consideration practice of clear communication contributed to positive counselor-manager relationships by facilitating openness and candor. While data associated with RQ1/theme 2 indicated that clear communication associated with inspirational motivation contributed to productivity, the present finding indicated that clear communication associated with individualized consideration contributed to positive counselor-manager relationships. This finding was consistent with conclusions associated with transformational leadership indicating that candid, clear, and frequent leader communications with employees are important means of meeting employees' individual needs and supporting their self-actualization (Breevaart & Bakker, 2018; Muchiri et al., 2019).

Findings in this study added to those of previous researchers by indicating that in mental health care research settings, participants perceived individualized consideration based on clear communication as effective in improving the quality of counselor-manager relationships because it facilitated constructive transparency about the counselors' performance and managerial openness to counselors' feedback about needs and ideas.

RQ3. From the perspective of counselors and managers, what transactional managerial tactics produce positive work outcomes? Three major themes emerged during data analysis to answer this question. The first relevant theme was: Participants feel that transactional leadership contributes to employee independence and confidence. In relation to this theme, participant responses were based on their perceptions that transactional leadership is a hands-off approach in which the manager defines a task, states the reward for success, and then leaves the employee to complete the task autonomously. Counselors who contributed to the theme did not acknowledge the quid pro quo component of transactional leadership. This finding, therefore, diverged from previous literature in that it attributed the positive effects of transactional leadership on counselor independence and confidence to their exercise of significant autonomy and discretion. This perception of transactional leadership is significant because it contrasts with the findings of researchers such as Nazim (2016), Rawung, Wuryaningrat, and Elvinita, (2015), and Sheshi and Kercini (2017). These researchers attributed the positive effects of transactional leadership to the engagement of participants' self-interests through incentives. The finding that the perception of transactional leadership is effective because of its facilitation of counselor autonomy added to the previous literature that counselor autonomy, rather than engagement of self-interest through rewards, was the significant factor in improving counselors' confidence and independence.

The second relevant theme used to answer RQ3 was: Participants feel that offering rewards or punishments to employees promotes positive outcomes. In contrast to the previous theme, data associated with this theme referred explicitly to the reward component of transactional leadership. Managers reported that incentives such as vacation days, overtime pay, and monetary incentives for obtaining certification were effective in increasing desired counselor behaviors in the short term. This finding was consistent with those of researchers such as Nazim (2016), Rawung, Wuryaningrat, and Elvinita, (2015), and Sheshi and Kercini (2017), who identified incentivization as an effective means of promoting desired behaviors. The finding in this study added to the previous literature by confirming the effectiveness of incentives in a previously unexplored context, and by adding that incentives have limited efficacy in improving desired behaviors among counselors. Specifically, manager participants described transactional incentives as producing the desired behavior only for as long as the incentive was available. When the incentive was no longer available, the desired behavior stopped. Manager participants perceived transformational leadership as more effective in producing long-term changes in counselors' performance.

The third theme relevant to answering RQ3 was: Participants feel that transactional leadership contributes to increased employee effectiveness. Like the previous theme, this finding indicated that rewards are effective in producing desired manager behaviors in the research settings, in agreement with the findings of researchers such as Nazim (2016), Rawung, Wuryaningrat, and Elvinita (2015), and Sheshi and Kercini

(2017). However, in characterizing the effects of transactional strategies on counselors' effectiveness, managers conflated incentives for skill acquisition and incentives for increasing the volume of the workload in which previously acquired skills were applied. The reported long-term effects of incentives on employee effectiveness varied according to the specific behavior being rewarded. When skill acquisition was incentivized, the skill was retained in the long term, even though additional incentives for its application were not offered. When increased application of existing skills was incentivized, as when counselors were rewarded for drastically increasing their caseloads, the continuation of the behavior remained contingent on the continuation of the incentive.

These findings confirmed those of Masa'deh et al. (2016) that transactional leadership is effective in promoting knowledge sharing and acquisition, and the finding of Sheshi and Kercini (2017) that transactional leadership is effective in increasing motivation. Findings in this study added to those of previous researchers that in the mental health care research settings, long-term effects of transactional incentives are differentiated according to the behaviors being incentivized. Elevated performance levels were dependent on the continuation of incentives, but skills persisted beyond the discontinuation of incentives for their acquisition.

RQ4. From the perspective of counselors and managers, what transactional managerial tactics produce positive relationships between the counselor and the manager? The theme that emerged to answer this research question was: Participants feel that transactional leadership tactics are less effective. Data associated with this theme indicated that within mental health care research settings specifically, transactional leadership was detrimental to counselor-manager relationships.

Participants suggested that transactional leadership could appear as a managerial invalidation of the intrinsic motivation counselors needed to perform well, that transactional leadership could cause counselors to feel neglected or punished by their supervisors, and that transactional leadership could become a form of leading by example that would influence counselors to develop transactional relationships with their clients. These findings were contrary to those of previous researchers such as Francis (2017), Taylor (2017), and Van Wart (2013), who argued that admixtures of transactional leadership strategies did not undermine the outcomes of transformational leadership in a business setting. Findings in the present study disputed those findings in the mental health care research settings, indicating that transactional strategies were likely to be damaging to both counselor-manager and counselor-client relationships. A possible explanation for this discrepancy with the previous literature may be that for-profit business is inherently transactional. Job commitment and performance may not require significant levels of intrinsic motivation, and strong emotional connections with clients and customers may be less productive than purely transactional relationships.

Recommendations for Practice

The first recommendation for practice is based on the finding that transformational leadership involving inspirational motivation is effective in mental health care research settings in improving employee morale, productivity, and retention. This finding was consistent with previous literature indicating that inspirational motivation has these effects. As Breevaart and Bakker (2018) and Muchiri et al. (2019) found, and as was confirmed in this study, inspirational motivation can improve employee motivation and commitment by facilitating the alignment of individual and collective goals. In mental health care settings specifically, managers' communications about collective, organizational goals should be explicit, consistent, and clear, a finding consistent with those of researchers in business contexts (e.g., Afsar et al., 2017; Antonakis & Day, 2017). Participants in this study suggested that assuming the goals of counseling were sufficiently communicated by the job specifications led to lower employee morale and engagement, possibly as a result of goal setting of this kind being individual and prescriptive rather than voluntary and collective. In relation to the elevated levels of burnout and turnover among counselors described in previous literature (e.g., Holman et al., 2018; Quintana & Cabrera, 2015; Schilling et al., 2018), findings in this study suggested that managers' clear, consistent articulation of a vision for collective achievement provided sufficient orientation and inspiration to sustain employee commitment and reduce burnout and attrition.

The second recommendation for practice emerged from the finding that transformational leadership involving individualized consideration was effective in creating positive counselor-manager relationships. This finding was consistent with those of previous researchers such as Breevaart and Bakker (2018) and Gable (2012). But it added the implication for practice that individualized consideration in the mental health care research should have a specific focus. First, managers should focus on encouraging and supporting counselors. Practices for encouraging counselors could include emails with praise for specific achievements and personalized verbal recognition of strong performance. Second, managers should provide clear, candid critiques of counselors' performances in relation to clearly defined collective goals and standards. These practices contributed to positive counselor-manager relationships by maintaining openness and constructive transparency. They also contributed to employee morale through recognition of high performance and removal of ambiguity about performance quality overall.

The third recommendation for practice emerged from the study's findings that transactional leadership in the mental health care research settings had positive long-term effects on skill acquisition and maintenance. Participants reported that transactional strategies were effective in incentivizing counselors' pursuits of certification and acquisitions of specific skills. These gains, by their nature, persisted after the incentive was discontinued. This finding was consistent with that of Masa'deh et al. (2016), that transactional leadership is effective in promoting knowledge sharing and acquisition. The practical implication in mental health care settings is that monetary incentives may be effective in encouraging counselors to acquire credentials and skills that will be assets to the counselors themselves and to their employing organizations. No negative short- or long-term effects were associated with the transactional practice of incentivizing skill and credential acquisition for counselors.

The fourth recommendation for practice is based on the findings that transactional incentives are likely to have positive short-term effects on performance but may have negative long-term effects on counselor-manager and counselor-client relationships. Findings that transactional incentives are effective in increasing performance while the incentive is available were consistent with those of Nazim (2016), Rawung, Wuryaningrat, and Elvinita, (2015), and Sheshi and Kercini (2017). However, it was also found in this study that transactional leadership could appear as a managerial invalidation of the intrinsic motivation counselors needed to perform well, that transactional leadership could cause counselors to feel neglected or punished by their supervisors, and that it could become a form of leading by example that would influence counselors to develop transactional relationships with their clients.

The practical implication of this finding is that the long-term effects of broad application of transactional strategies in a mental health care setting are likely to be negative. Transformational leadership is more effective in producing long-term improvements in performance and counselor-manager relationships. Practitioners should therefore consider confining transactional strategies to incentivizing skill and credential acquisition, while relying on transformational strategies to increase performance volume and quality.

Recommendations for Future Research

The first recommendation emerges from the methodological limitations of this study. Qualitative research is unable to yield generalizable or objective results. To address this limitation, it is recommended that future researchers undertake quantitative studies involving a large sample to facilitate generalization. It is recommended that such research be conducted to assess the agreement of the findings in this study with the perceptions of a generalizable sample of mental health care managers and counselors.

Additionally, the findings in this study included a number of influences that participants perceived between manager behaviors and counselor experiences and performances. Although these findings were consistent with causal relationships identified in the work of researchers in business contexts, such as those of Breevaart and Bakker (2018) and Muchiri et al. (2019), it is recommended that quantitative research using an experimental design be undertaken specifically in mental health care settings to test whether the influences described in the present findings correspond to objective, generalizable causal relationships.

The second recommendation for future research is based on the design limitations of this study. The findings in this study were based on participants' self-reports. Identification of themes across multiple participants minimized the potential influence of inaccuracies or distortions in individual participant responses. It is recommended that future researchers assess the credibility of the findings through qualitative case study research involving data streams that are independent of participant self-reports. Such data streams might include researcher observations and analysis of archival data. The findings from such research would contribute to a more robust range of evidence for the findings in the present study, or to the modification of the present findings to encompass a wider range of sources and perspectives.

The third recommendation for future research is associated with the finding in this study that transformational leadership is more effective than a transactional style in the mental health care research settings, and that transactional leadership might even be damaging in the long term. This finding conflicted with those of researchers such as Nazim (2016), Rawung, Wuryaningrat, and Elvinita (2015), and Sheshi and Kercini (2017), although it is likely that differences between for-profit business contexts and mental health care contexts account for the discrepancy. However, mental health care practitioners would likely benefit from clear, evidence-based guidance regarding the optimal scope of transactional leadership in mental health care settings. It is therefore recommended that future quantitative and qualitative research be undertaken to assess the generalizability of the finding in the present study and to further refine it to facilitate development of more specific evidence-based guidance for practitioners.

Conclusion

The purpose of this qualitative research was to explore how transactional and transformational leadership styles influence the counselor-manager relationship in mental health counseling settings. This study was conducted to address the problem that, although there is a significant body of research on leadership in business contexts (Smith & Khojasteh, 2014), there is a gap in the literature regarding the leadership relationship between counselors and managers in the mental health field (Bowen & Moore, 2014). The conceptual framework in this study was drawn from the literature on transformational and transactional leadership styles.

Findings indicated that mental health care workers perceived the transformational leadership style as more effective than the transactional style. Participants perceived the inspirational motivation component of transformational leadership as effective in increasing counselor productivity, morale, and retention. Participants perceived individualized consideration as conducive to positive counselor-manager relationships. Transactional leadership was perceived as effective for promoting short-term productivity, as well as for promoting skill and credential acquisition that would have long-term benefits. However, transactional leadership was perceived as potentially detrimental to long-term counselor-manager and counselor-client relationships.

The most significant recommendation for practice to emerge from this study was associated with the finding that participant experiences of transactional leadership in their mental health care settings were inconsistent with the findings of researchers working in business contexts. Transactional leadership practices, in which performance is motivated by the expectation of quid pro quo rewards, may be effective in an inherently transactional context such as for-profit business, in which high performance may not require strong, intrinsic motivation in which transactional relationships with clients and customers may be more conducive to success than creating strong emotional bonds.

In a mental health care setting, counseling success is largely predicated on a counselor's willingness and ability to form meaningful bonds of empathy and trust with clients. Although it may be possible to incentivize caseload increases or overtime work with rewards, meaningful bonding with individual clients may require intrinsic motivation. If intrinsic motivation is needed, then transactional incentives such as vacation days or bonus pay may be effective for increasing metrics such as caseload quantity, but they are unlikely to improve service quality or client outcomes. Overall, findings indicated that transformational leadership, with its emphasis on inspiring employees to contribute to a clear, collective vision while meeting employees' individual needs for support, encouragement, and self-actualization, is better suited than transactional strategies to ensuring that counselors are truly dedicated to meeting client needs.

REFERENCES

Afsar, B., Badir, Y. F., Saeed, B. B., & Hafeez, S. (2017). Transformational and transactional leadership and employee's entrepreneurial behavior in knowledge-intensive industries. *International Journal of Human Resource Management, 28*(2), 307–332. DOI: 10.1080/09585192.2016.1244893.

Afsar, B., & Umrani, W. A. (2019). Transformational leadership and innovative work behavior. *European Journal of Innovation Management, 1460–1060.* DOI:10.1108/EJIM-12-2018-0257/full/html.

Afshari, L., & Gibson, P. (2016). How to increase organizational commitment through transactional leadership. *Leadership & Organization Development Journal, 37*(4), 507–519.

Ahmad, F., Abbas, T., Latif, S., & Rasheed, A. (2014). Impact of transformational leadership on employee motivation in telecommunication sector. *Journal of Management Policies and Practices, 2*(2), 11–25.

Alban-Metcalfe, J. (2018). Engaging leadership—a better approach to leading a team? *Nursing Times, 114*(6), 21–24.

Allio, R. J. (2016). Learning to be a leader. *Strategy & Leadership, 44*(4), 3–9.

American Mental Health Counselors Association. (2019). *AMHCA*. Retrieved from https://www.amhca.org/home.

Andersen, L. B., Bjørnholt, B., Bro, L. L., & Holm-Petersen, C. (2018). Achieving high quality through transformational leadership: A qualitative multilevel analysis of transformational leadership and perceived professional quality. *Public Personnel Management, 47*(1), 51–72. DOI:10.1177/0091026017747270.

Antonakis, J., & Day, D. V. (eds.) (2017). *The Nature of Leadership*. Sage Publications, 175–178.

Archibald, R. D., & Archibald, S. (2016). *Leading and Managing Innovation: What Every Executive Team Must Know about Project, Program, and Portfolio Management*. Auerbach Publications, 35–36.

Arthur, S., Herring, N., Morrison, L., & Bertsch, A. (2017). Jack Welch: The bridge between Drucker and Goleman. *International Journal of Business and Social Science, 8*(3).

Attar, M., Jami, M. S., & Kalfaoğlu, S. (2019). Effect of cultural intelligence on and transformational leadership styles: A research in charity organizations in Erbil. *Selcuk Üniversitesi Sosyal Bilimler Enstitüsü Dergisi, 41*, 148–160. Retrieved from http://search.proquest.com.proxy1.ncu.edu/docview/2237780665?accountid=28180.

Ayoub, J. J., Abiad, M., Forman, M. R., Honein-AbouHaidar, G., & Naja, F. (2018). The interaction of personal, contextual, and study characteristics and their effect on recruitment and participation of pregnant women in research: a qualitative study in Lebanon. *BMC Medical Research Methodology, 18*(1), 155. DOI:10.1186/s12874-018-0616-5.

Bailey, J. (2008). First steps in qualitative data analysis: Transcribing. *Family Practice, 25*(2), 127–131. DOI: 10.1093/fampra/cmn003.

Bailey, K. (2008). *Methods of Social Research*. Simon and Schuster.

Barreto, N. B., & Hogg, M. A. (2018). Influence and leadership in small groups: Impact of group prototypicality, social status, and task competence. *Journal of Theoretical Social Psychology, 2*(1), 26–33.

Bass, B., & Avolio, B. (1995). *MLQ multifactor leadership questionnaire*. Mind Garden.

Bealer, D., & Bhanugopan, R. (2014). Transactional and transformational leadership behavior of expatriate and national managers in the UAE: A cross-cultural comparative analysis. *International Journal of Human Resource Management, 25*(2), 293–316. DOI:10.1080/0 9585192.2013.826914.

Bengtsson, M. (2016). How to plan and perform a qualitative study using thematic analysis. *NursingPlus Open, 2,* 8–14. DOI:10.1016/j.npls.2016.01.001.

Bennett, D. (2018). The relationship between transactional and transformational leadership attributes and organizational performance in the Caribbean. *International Journal of Education and Management Studies, 8*(4), 446–451. Retrieved from http://search.proquest.com.proxy1.ncu. edu/docview/2218169202?accountid=28180.

Bhugra, D., Ruiz, P., & Gupta, S. (eds.). (2013). *Leadership in Psychiatry*. Wiley Blackwell, 35.

Birasnav, M. (2014). Knowledge management and organizational performance in the service industry: The role of transformational leadership beyond the effects of transactional leadership. *Journal of Business Research*, 67(8), 1622–1629. DOI:10.1016/j.jbusres.2013.09.006.

Bonsu, S., & Twum-Danso, E. (2018). Leadership style in the global economy: A focus on cross-cultural and transformational leadership. *Journal of Marketing & Management*, 9(2), 37.

Braun, V., & Clarke, V. (2008). Using thematic analysis in psychology. *Qualitative Research in Psychology*, 3(2), 77–101. DOI:10.1191/1478088706qp063oa.

Breevaart, K., & Bakker, A. B. (2018). Daily job demands and employee work engagement: The role of daily transformational leadership behavior. *Journal of Occupational Health Psychology*, 23(3), 338–349. DOI:10.1037/ocp0000082.

Breevaart, K., Bakker, A., Hetland, J., Demerouti, E., Olsen, O. K., & Espevik, R. (2014). Daily transactional and transformational leadership and daily employee engagement. *Journal of Occupational and Organizational Psychology*, 87(1), 138–157. DOI:10.1111/joop.12041.

Byrne, A., Crossan, M., & Seijts, G. (2018). The development of leader character through crucible moments. *Journal of Management Education*, 42(2), 265–293. DOI:1 0.1177/1052562917717292.

Cartwright, R. (2017). Mastering team leadership. Macmillan International Higher Education.

Castlebarry, A., & Nolen, A. (2018). Thematic analysis of qualitative research data: Is it easy as it sounds? *Currents in Pharmacy Teaching and Learning*, 10, 807–815. DOI:10.1016/j.cptl.2018.03.109.

Clarke, S. (2013). Safety leadership: A meta-analytic review of transformational and transactional leadership styles as antecedents of safety behaviors. *Journal of Occupational and Organizational Psychology*, *86*(1), 22–49. DOI: 0.1111/j.2044-8325.2012.02064.x.

Clipa, O., & Greciuc, Ş. M.-A. (2018). Relations of style of leadership and achievement motivation for teacher. *Romanian Journal for Multidimensional Education/ Revista Romaneasca Pentru Educatie Multidimensional*, *10*(4), 55–64. DOI:10.18662/rrem/7.

Corrigan, P. W., Diwan, S., Campion, J., & Rashid, F. (2002). Transformational leadership and the mental health team. *Administration and Policy in Mental Health and Mental Health Services Research*, *30*(2), 97–108. DOI:10.1023/A:1022569617123.

Cranny-Francis, A., Waring, W., Stavropoulos, P., & Kirkby, J. (2017). *Gender Studies: Terms and Debates*. Macmillan International Higher Education.

Cristancho, S. M., Goldszmidt, M., Lingard, L., & Watling, C. (2018). Qualitative research essentials for medical education. *Singapore Medical Journal*, *59*(12), 622–627. DOI:10.11622/smedj.2018093.

Cummings, T. G. (2017). Warren G. Bennis: Generous Company: Generous Company. *The Palgrave Handbook of Organizational Change Thinkers*, 1–15. DOI:10.1007/978-3-319-49820.

Dai, Y. D., Dai, Y. Y., Chen, K. Y., & Wu, H. C. (2013). Transformational vs. transactional leadership: which is better? A study on employees of international tourist hotels in Taipei City. *International Journal of Contemporary Hospitality Management*, *25*(5), 760–778. DOI:10.1108/IJCHM-09-2015-0490/full/html.

Data US. (2018). *Counselor Demographics*. Retrieved from: https://datausa.io/profile/soc/counselors.

De Meuse, K. P. (2019). A meta-analysis of the relationship between learning agility and leader success. *Journal of Organizational Psychology,* *19*(1). DOI:10.33423.jop. v19i.1088.

Denzin, N. K., & Lincoln, Y. S. (2011). *The SAGE handbook of qualitative research* (4th ed.). Thousand Oaks, CA: Sage.

Dolph, D. A. (2017). Problem-solving tips for school business officials. *School Business Affairs, 83*(2). Retrieved from: https://ecommons.udayton.edu/eda_fac_pub/215/.

Duemer, L. S. (2017). A history of transactional leadership in academe: A cautionary tale. *Journal of Philosophy & History of Education, 67,* xxxv–xlii. Retrieved from https://search-ebscohost-com.proxy1.ncu.edu/login. aspx?direct=true&db=ehh&AN=129722653&site= eds-live.

Epitropaki, O., Kark, R., Mainemelis, C., & Lord, R. G. (2017). Leadership and followership identity processes: A multilevel review. *The Leadership Quarterly, 28*(1), 104–129. DOI:10.1016/j.leaqua.2016.10.003.

Esty, D. C., & Bell, M. L. (2018). Business leadership in global climate change responses. *American Journal of Public Health, 108,* S80–S84. DOI:10.2105/ AJPH.2018.304336.

Fusch, P. I., & Ness, L. R. (2015). Are we there yet? Data saturation in qualitative research. *The Qualitative Report, 20*(9), 1408. Retrieved from https://nsuworks. nova.edu/tqr/vol20/iss9/3/.

Gabel, S. (2012). Demoralization in mental health organizations: Leadership and social support help. *Psychiatric Quarterly, 83*(4), 489–496. DOI:10.1007/s11126-012-9217-3.

Ghani, F. A., Derani, N. E. S., Aznam, N., Mohamad, N., Zakaria, S. A. A., & Toolib, S. N. (2018). An empirical investigation of the relationship between transformational, transactional female leadership styles and employee engagement. *Global Business and Management Research, 10*(3), 724. Retrieved from https://search-ebscohost-com.proxy1.ncu.edu/login.aspx?direct=true&db=bth&AN=133618166&site=eds-live.

Glesne, C. (2016). *Becoming Qualitative Researchers: An Introduction*. Upper Saddle River, NJ: Pearson.

Fischer, S. A. (2016). Transformational leadership in nursing: a concept analysis. *Journal of Advanced Nursing, 72*(11), 2644–2653. DOI:10.1111/jan.13049.

Francis, U. C. (2017). Transformational and transactional leadership styles among leaders of administrative ministries in Lagos, Nigeria. *IFE PsychologIA, 25*(2), 151–164.

Frick, W. C., Gross, S. J., & Wilson, A. S. (2018). Being an ethical leader means taking responsibility for students' academic and social success. In *Developing Ethical Principles for School Leadership* (pp. 1–27). Routledge.

Ford, J., Harding, N. H., Gilmore, S., & Richardson, S. (2017). Becoming the leader: Leadership as material presence. *Organization Studies, 38*(11), 1553–1571. DOI:10.1177/0170840616677633.

Gabel, S. (2013). Transformational leadership and health care. *Medical Science Educator, 23*(1), 55–60. DOI:10.111/jan.13049.

Ghani, F. A., Derani, N. E. S., Aznam, N., Mohamad, N., Zakaria, S. A. A., & Toolib, S. N. (2018). An empirical investigation of the relationship between transformational, transactional female leadership styles and employee engagement. *Global Business and Management Research, 10*(3), 724.

Giltinane, C. L. (2013). Leadership styles and theories. *Nursing Standard, 27*(41). Retrieved from https://www.taylorfrancis.com/books/e/9781315695792/chapters/10.4324/9781315695792-2.

Golley, C., Quezada, A., Myers, R., & Smith, W. (2018). *The Effect of Leadership Traits and Training on the Effectiveness of a Team.* Retrieved from: https://commons.erau.edu/pr-discovery-day/2018/posters-and-presentations-demonstrations/39/.

Grabo, A., Spisak, B. R., & van Vugt, M. (2017). Charisma as signal: An evolutionary perspective on charismatic leadership. *The Leadership Quarterly, 28*(4), 473–485. DOI:10.1016/j.leaqua.2017.05.001.

Hamstra, M. R., Van Yperen, N. W., Wisse, B., & Sassenberg, K. (2014). Transformational and transactional leadership and followers' achievement goals. *Journal of Business and Psychology, 29*(3), 413–425. Retrieved from: https://www.frontiersin.org/articles/10.3389/fpsyg.2017.01754/full. DOI:http://dx.doi.org.proxy1.ncu.edu/10.1007/s10869-013-9322-9.

Hargett, C. W., Doty, J. P., Hauck, J. N., Webb, A. M., Cook, S. H., Tsipis, N. E., ... & Taylor, D. C. (2017). Developing a model for effective leadership in health care: A concept mapping approach. *Journal of Healthcare Leadership, 9*, 69. DOI:10.2147/JHL.S141664.

Hartzler-Weakley, K. (2018). *Examining the Impact of Transformational and Transactional Leadership Style on Work Attitudes, Motivation, and Work Outcomes in Nonprofit Organizations* (order no. 10837902). Available from ProQuest Dissertations & Theses Global. (2090744014).

Retrieved from http://search.proquest.com.proxy1.ncu. edu/docview/2090744014?accountid=28180.

Haselhuhn, M. P., Wong, E. M., & Ormiston, M. E. (2017). With great power comes shared responsibility: Psychological power and the delegation of authority. *Personality and Individual Differences, 108*, 1–4. DOI:10.1016/j.paid.2016.11.052.

Heok, K. (2010). Leadership in psychiatry: Training future leaders. *Asia-Pacific Psychiatry, 2*(4), 173–174. DOI:10.1111/j.1758-5872.2010.00085.x.

Hesler, E. J. 2018. The mental health workforce: A primer. *Congressional Research Service.* Retrieved from: www. fas.org/sgp/crs/misc/R43255.pdf.

Higgs, M., & Dulewicz, V. (2016). Developments in leadership thinking. In *Leading with Emotional Intelligence* (pp. 75–103). Palgrave Macmillan, Cham.

Holman, L. F., Watts, R., Robles-Pina, R., & Grubbs, L. (2018). Exploration of potential predictor variables leading to school counselor burnout. *Journal of School Counseling, 16*(9), 1–29. Retrieved from https://search-ebscohost-com.proxy1.ncu.edu/login.aspx?direct=true &db=ehh&AN=132546667&site=eds-live.

Holten, A. L., Bøllingtoft, A., Carneiro, I. G., & Borg, V. (2018). A within-country study of leadership perceptions and outcomes across native and immigrant employees: Questioning the universality of transformational leadership. *Journal of Management & Organization, 24*(1), 145–162. Retrieved from: https://www.cambridge.org/core/journals/journal-of-management-and-organization/article/withincountry-study-of-leadership-perceptions-and-outcomes-across-native-and-immigrant-employees-questioning-

the-universality-of-transformational-leadership/
F058646A109F5EDDB25D991A8C3A9E99.

Jacobs, S. M. A., & Kushner, R. S. (2017). *How Can You Become the Boss? From Personal Mastery to Organizational Transformation*. Rowman & Littlefield.

Jakobsen, R., & Sørlie, V. (2016). Ethical challenges: Trust and leadership in dementia care. *Nursing Ethics, 23*(6), 636–645. DOI:10.1177/0969733015580810.

Jensen, U. T., Andersen, L. B., Bro, L. L., Bøllingtoft, A., Eriksen, T. L. M., Holten, A.-L., … Würtz, A. (2019). Conceptualizing and measuring transformational and transactional leadership. *Administration & Society, 51*(1), 3–33. https://doi-org.proxy1.ncu. edu/10.1177/0095399716667157.

Jones, E. L., & Jones, R. C. (2017). Leadership style and career success of women leaders in nonprofit organizations. *Advancing Women in Leadership, 37*, 37–48. Retrieved from http://search.proquest.com.proxy1.ncu.edu/ docview/1988004189?accountid=28180.

Kang, S., & Svensson, P. G. (2018). Shared leadership in sport for development and peace: A conceptual framework of antecedents and outcomes. *Sport Management Review*. https://doi-org.proxy1.ncu.edu/10.1016/j. smr.2018.06.010.

Karagianni, D., & Jude Montgomery, A. (2018). Developing leadership skills among adolescents and young adults: a review of leadership programmes. *International Journal of Adolescence and Youth, 23*(1), 86–98. DOI:10.1080/02 673843.2017.1292928.

Kim, S., & Shin, M. (2017). The effectiveness of transformational leadership on empowerment. *Cross*

Cultural & Strategic Management, 24(2), 271–287. DOI:1108/CCSM-03-2016-0075.

Koeslag-Kreunen, M. G., Van der Klink, M. R., Van den Bossche, P., & Gijselaers, W. H. (2018). Leadership for team learning: The case of university teacher teams. *Higher Education, 75*(2), 191–207. DOI:10.1007/s10734-017-0126-0.

Korstjens, I., & Moser, A. (2018). Series: Practical guidance to qualitative research. Part 4: Trustworthiness and publishing. *The European Journal of General Practice, 24*(1), 120–124. https://doi-org.proxy1.ncu.edu/10.1080/13814788.2017.1375092.

Krepia, V., Katsaragakis, S., Kaitelidou, D., & Prezerakos, P. (2018). Transformational leadership and its evolution in nursing. *Progress in Health Sciences, 8*(1). Retrieved from https://www.umb.edu.pl/photo/pliki/progress-file/phs/phs_2018_1/189-194_krepia_.pdf.

Krippendorff, K. (2018). *Thematic Analysis: An Introduction to Its Methodology* (pp. 128–130). Sage.

Martin, J. (2015). Transformational and transactional leadership: An exploration of gender, experience, and institution type. *Portal: Libraries and the Academy, 15*(2), 331–351. DOI:10.1353/pla.2015.0015.

Martin, J. A., Hamilton, B. E., Osterman, M. J., Curtin, S. C., & Mathews, T. J. (2015). Births: Final data for 2013.

Masa'deh, R., Obeidat, B. Y., & Tarhini, A. (2016). A Jordanian empirical study of the associations among transformational leadership, transactional leadership, knowledge sharing, job performance, and firm performance: A structural equation modelling approach. *The Journal of Management Development, 35*(5), 681–705.

Retrieved from http://search.proquest.com.proxy1.ncu.
edu/docview/1791345320?accountid=28180.

McCleskey, J. A. (2014). Situational, transformational, and
transactional leadership and leadership development.
Journal of Business Studies Quarterly, 5(4), 117.

Mihas, P. (2019). Qualitative data analysis. In *Oxford Research
Encyclopedia of Education* (pp. 45–47).

Mo, D., O'Hara, N. N., Hengel, R., Cheong, A. R., &
Singhal, A. (2019). The preferred attributes of a
trauma team leader: Evidence from a discrete choice
experiment. *Journal of surgical education, 76*(1), 120–126.
DOI:10.1016/j.surg.2018.06.021.

Morrison, M. A., & Lent, R. W. (2018). The working
alliance, beliefs about the supervisor, and counseling
self-efficacy: Applying the relational efficacy model to
counselor supervision. *Journal of Counseling Psychology,
65*(4), 512–522. DOI:10.1037/cou0000267.

Moye, N., Mueller-Hanson, R., & Langfred, C. (2017).
Assessment for leader development. *The Wiley Blackwell
Handbook of the Psychology of Recruitment, Selection and
Employee Retention*, 353–375.

Muchiri, M. K., McMurray, A. J., Nkhoma, M., & Pham,
H. C. (2019). How transformational and empowering
leader behaviors enhance workplace safety: A review
and research agenda. *Journal of Developing Areas, 53*(1),
257–265. DOI:10.1353/jda.2019.0015.

Nassaji, H. (2015). Qualitative and descriptive research: Data
type versus data analysis. *Language Teaching Research,
19*(2), 129–132. DOI:10.1177/1362168815572747.

Nawaz, Z. A. K. D. A., & Khan, I. (2016). Leadership theories
and styles: A literature review. *Leadership, 16*, 1–7.

Nazim, F. (2016). Principals' transformational and transactional leadership style and job satisfaction of college teachers. *Journal of Education and Practice, 7*(34), 18–22. Retrieved from https://search-ebscohost-com.proxy1.ncu.edu/login.aspx?direct=true&db=eric&AN=EJ1126682&site=eds-live.

Northouse, P. G. (2018). *Leadership: Theory and practice.* Sage.

Odumeru, J. A., & Ogbonna, I. G. (2013). Transformational vs. transactional leadership theories: Evidence in literature. *International Review of Management and Business Research, 2*(2), 355. Retrieved from: http://www.indianjournals.com/ijor.aspx?target=ijor:zijmr&volume=6&issue=2&article=016.

Olsen, G. W. (2017). Doctrine and power: Theological controversy and Christian leadership in the later roman empire. *The European Legacy,5(*1), 750–752. DOI:10.1080.10848770.2017.1326671.

Olten, A., Bøllingtoft, A., Carneiro, I. G., & Borg, V. (2018). A within-country study of leadership perceptions and outcomes across native and immigrant employees: Questioning the universality of transformational leadership. *Journal of Management and Organization, 24*(1), 145–162. DOI:1017/jmo.2017.2.

Peters, K., & Halcomb, E. (2015). Interviews in qualitative research. *Nurse Researcher (2014+), 22*(4), 6. DOI:10.7748/nr.22.4.6.s2.

Prasad, B., & Junni, P. (2016). CEO transformational and transactional leadership and organizational innovation: The moderating role of environmental dynamism. *Management Decision, 54*(7), 1542–1568. Retrieved from http://search.proquest.com.proxy1.ncu.edu/docview/1809013503?accountid=28180.

Rabionet, S. E. (2011). How I learned to design and conduct semi-structured interviews: An ongoing and continuous journey. *Qualitative Report, 16*(2), 563–566. Retrieved from https://eric.ed.gov/?id=EJ926305.

Ramos, D. G. G. (2017). Social media health interaction theory: A new theory for social media research: OJNI. *On-Line Journal of Nursing Informatics, 21*(2), 151–169. DOI:10.115.

Rawung, F. H., Wuryaningrat, N. F., & Elvinita, L. E. (2015). The influence of transformational and transactional leadership on knowledge sharing: An empirical study on small and medium businesses in Indonesia. *Asian Academy of Management Journal, 20*(1), 123–145.

Rodrigues, A. D. O., & Ferreira, M. C. (2015). The impact of transactional and transformational leadership style on organizational citizenship behaviors. *Psico-USF, 20*(3), 493–504.

Roller, M. R., & Lavrakas, P. J. (2018). A total quality framework approach to sharing qualitative research data: Comment on Dubois et al, (2018). *Qualitative Psychology, 5*(3), 394–401. DOI:10.1037/qup0000081.

Rosen, Christopher C., Lauren S. Simon, Ravi S. Gajendran, Russell E. Johnson, Hun Whee Lee, & Szu-Han Joanna Lin. (2018). Boxed in by your inbox: Implications of daily e-mail demands for managers' leadership behaviors. *Journal of Applied Psychology*.

Rosenbach, W. E. (2018). *Contemporary Issues in Leadership* (pp. 45–48). Routledge.

Rowold, J. (2014). Instrumental leadership: Extending the transformational-transactional leadership paradigm. *German Journal of Human Resource Management, 28*(3), 367–390.

Saeed, S. A., Silver, S., Buwalda, V. J., Khin, E. K., Petit, J. R., Mohyuddin, F., ... & Levin, S. (2018). Psychiatric management, administration, and leadership: A continuum or distinct concepts? *Psychiatric Quarterly, 89*(2), 315–328. DOI:10.1007/s11126-017-9536-5.

Sandelowski, M. (2010). What's in a name? Qualitative description revisited. *Research in Nursing & Health, 33*(1), 77–84. DOI:10.1002/nur.20362.

Saravo, B., Netzel, J., & Kiesewetter, J. (2017). The need for strong clinical leaders—Transformational and transactional leadership as a framework for resident leadership training. *Plos One, 12*(8), e0183019. DOI:1371/journal.pone.0183019.

Sassenberg, K., & Hamstra, M. R. W. (2017). The intrapersonal and interpersonal dynamics of self-regulation in the leadership process. In *Advances in Experimental Social Psychology,* vol. 55 (pp. 193–257). Academic Press.

Schilling, E. J., Randolph, M., & Boan-Lenzo, C. (2018). Job burnout in school psychology: How big is the problem? *Contemporary School Psychology, 22*(3), 324–331. DOI:10.1007/s40688-017-0138-x.

Sfantou, D., Laliotis, A., Patelarou, A., Sifaki-Pistolla, D., Matalliotakis, M., & Patelarou, E. (2017). Importance of leadership style towards quality of care measures in health care settings: a systematic review. *Healthcare Multidisciplinary Digital Publishing Institute, 17*(1), 117–129.

Shahhosseini, M., Silong, A. D., & Ismaill, I. A. (2013). Relationship between transactional, transformational leadership styles, emotional intelligence and job performance. *Researchers World, 4*(1), 15.

Shamir, B., & Eilam, G. (2005). "What's your story?" A life-stories approach to authentic leadership development. *The Leadership Quarterly, 16*(3), 395–417. DOI:10.1016/j.leaqua.2005.03.005.

Sheshi, A., & Kercini, D. (2017). The role of transactional, transformational and participative leadership in performance of SMEs in Albania. *Albanian Journal of Agricultural Sciences,* 285–292.

Silverman, D. (ed.). (2016). *Qualitative Research.* Boston: Sage.

Singh, S. P. (2000). Running an effective community mental health team. *Advances in Psychiatric Treatment, 6*(6), 414–422.

Smith, C. (2015). Exemplary leadership: How style and culture predict organizational outcomes. *Nursing Management, 46*(3), 47–51.

Smith, J. W., & Khojasteh, M. (2014). Use of humor in the workplace. *International Journal of Management & Information Systems (IJMIS), 18*(1), 71–78. Retrieved from https://clutejournals.com/index.php/IJMIS/article/view/8340.

Smith, M. J., Young, D. J., Figgins, S. G., & Arthur, C. A. (2017). Transformational leadership in elite sport: A qualitative analysis of effective leadership behaviors in cricket. *Sport Psychologist, 31*(1), 1. Retrieved from https://search-ebscohost-com.proxy1.ncu.edu/login.aspx?direct=true&db=edb&AN=122236620&site=eds-live.

Sorsa, M. A., Kiikkala, I., & Åstedt-Kurki, P. (2015). Bracketing as a skill in conducting unstructured qualitative interviews. *Nurse Researcher, 22*(4). Retrieved from: pubmed.ncbi.nlm.nih.gov/25783146

Sousa, M. J., & Rocha, Á. (2019). Leadership styles and skills developed through game-based learning. *Journal of Business Research, 94,* 360–366. DOI:10.1016/j.jbsures.2018.0157.

Strandburg-Peshkin, A., Papageorgiou, D., Crofoot, M. C., & Farine, D. R. (2018). Inferring influence and leadership in moving animal groups. *Philosophical Transactions of the Royal Society B: Biological Sciences, 373*(1746). DOI:10.20170006.

Stuckey, H. L. (2015). The second step in data analysis: Coding qualitative research data. *Journal of Social Health and Diabetes, 3*(1), 007-010. DOI:10.4103/2321-0656.140875.

Substance Abuse Mental Health Services Administration (SAMHSA). (2019). *Mental Health.* Retrieved from https://www.samhsa.gov/.

Tang, K. N. (2019). Team development. In *Leadership and Change Management* (pp. 37–46). Springer, Singapore.

Taylor, J. (2017). Management of Australian water utilities: The significance of transactional and Transformational leadership. *Australian Journal of Public Administration, 76*(1), 18–32. DOI:10.1111/1467-8500.12200.

Taylor, S. E. (2006). Tend and befriend: Biobehavioral bases of affiliation under stress. *Current Directions in Psychological Science, 15*(6), 273–277. DOI:10.1111/j.1467-8721.2006.00451.x.

Tracy, S. J. (2019). *Qualitative Research Methods: Collecting Evidence, Crafting Analysis, Communicating Impact.* John Wiley & Sons.

Trahar, S. (ed.). (2006). *Narrative Research on Learning: Comparative and International Perspectives.* Symposium Books Ltd.

Tyssen, A. K., Wald, A., & Spieth, P. (2014). The challenge of transactional and transformational leadership in projects. *International Journal of Project Management, 32*(3), 365–375.

Ugwu, L. I., Enwereuzor, I. K., & Orji, E. U. (2016). Is trust in leadership a mediator between transformational leadership and in-role performance among small-scale factory workers? *Review of Managerial Science, 10*(4), 629–648. DOI:10.1007/s11846-015-0170-z.

Vaismoradi, M., Turunen, H., & Bondas, T. (2013). Thematic analysis and thematic analysis: Implications for conducting a qualitative descriptive study. *Nursing & Health Sciences, 15*(3), 398–405.

Van Dierendonck, D., Stam, D., Boersma, P., De Windt, N., & Alkema, J. (2014). Same difference? Exploring the differential mechanisms linking servant leadership and transformational leadership to follower outcomes. *The Leadership Quarterly, 25*(3), 544–562.

Van Knippenberg, D., & Sitkin, S. B. (2013). A critical assessment of charismatic—transformational leadership research: Back to the drawing board? *The Academy of Management Annals, 7*(1), 1–60.

Vänni, K. J., Neupane, S., & Nygård, C.-H. (2017). Associations between perceived leadership and presenteeism in an industrial population. *Occupational Medicine (Oxford, England), 67*(9), 672–677. DOI:10.1093/occmed/kqx156.

Vesso, S., & Alas, R. (2016). Characteristics of a coaching culture in leadership style the leader's impact on culture. *Problems and Perspectives in Management, 14*(2), 306–318. Retrieved from: https://businessperspectives.org/

images/pdf/applications/publishing/templates/article/assets/7192/PPM_2016_02cont2_Vesso.pdf.

Vito, G., E. Higgins, G., & S. Denney, A. (2014). Transactional and transformational leadership: An examination of the leadership challenge model. *Policing: An International Journal of Police Strategies & Management*, *37*(4), 809–822.

Watkins, M. D. (2016). Leading the team, you inherit. *Harvard Business Review*, *94*(6), 60–67. Retrieved from: https://www.apdata.com/upload/file/Edition_June_2016.pdf.

Yahaya, R., & Ebrahim, F. (2016). Leadership styles and organizational commitment: Literature review. *The Journal of Management Development*, *35*(2), 190–216. Retrieved from http://search.proquest.com.proxy1.ncu.edu/docview/1767544209?accountid=28180.

Yasin Ghadi, M., Fernando, M., & Caputi, P. (2013). Transformational leadership and work engagement: The mediating effect of meaning in work. *Leadership & Organization Development Journal*, *34*(6), 532–550.

Yin, R. K. (2013). Validity and generalization in future case study evaluations. *Evaluation*, *19*(3), 321–332. DOI:10.1177/1356389013497081.

Zamawe, F. C. (2015). The implication of using NVivo software in qualitative data analysis: Evidence-based reflections. *Malawi Medical Journal*, *27*(1), 13–15. Retrieved from https://www.ajol.info/index.php/mmj/article/view/116229.

Zeb, A., Saeed, G., Rehman, S. ur, Ullah, H., & Rabi, F. (2015). Transformational and transactional leadership styles and its impact on the performance of the public sector organizations in Pakistan. *Abasyn University Journal of Social Sciences*, *8*(1), 37–46.